THE TRAINER'S HANDBOOK OF LEADERSHIP DEVELOPMENT

About Pfeiffer

Pfeiffer serves the professional development and hands-on resource needs of training and human resource practitioners and gives them products to do their jobs better. We deliver proven ideas and solutions from experts in HR development and HR management, and we offer effective and customizable tools to improve workplace performance. From novice to seasoned professional, Pfeiffer is the source you can trust to make yourself and your organization more successful.

Essential Knowledge Pfeiffer produces insightful, practical, and comprehensive materials on topics that matter the most to training and HR professionals. Our Essential Knowledge resources translate the expertise of seasoned professionals into practical, how-to guidance on critical workplace issues and problems. These resources are supported by case studies, worksheets, and job aids and are frequently supplemented with CD-ROMs, websites, and other means of making the content easier to read, understand, and use.

Essential Tools Pfeiffer's Essential Tools resources save time and expense by offering proven, ready-to-use materials—including exercises, activities, games, instruments, and assessments—for use during a training or team-learning event. These resources are frequently offered in looseleaf or CD-ROM format to facilitate copying and customization of the material.

Pfeiffer also recognizes the remarkable power of new technologies in expanding the reach and effectiveness of training. While e-hype has often created whizbang solutions in search of a problem, we are dedicated to bringing convenience and enhancements to proven training solutions. All our e-tools comply with rigorous functionality standards. The most appropriate technology wrapped around essential content yields the perfect solution for today's on-the-go trainers and human resource professionals.

Pfeiffer
www.pfeiffer.com

Essential resources for training and HR professionals

THE TRAINER'S HANDBOOK OF LEADERSHIP DEVELOPMENT

Tools, Techniques, and Activities

Karen Lawson

Pfeiffer
A Wiley Imprint
www.pfeiffer.com

Published by Pfeiffer
An Imprint of Wiley
989 Market Street, San Francisco, CA 94103-1741 www.pfeiffer.com

Library of Congress Cataloging-in-Publication Data

Lawson, Karen.
  The trainer's handbook of leadership development : tools, techniques, and activities / Karen Lawson.
    p. cm.
  Includes bibliographical references and index.
  ISBN 978-0-470-88603-8 (pbk.)
    1. Leadership—Study and teaching.   I. Title.
  HD57.7.L383   2011
  658.4'07124—dc23

                                                                          2011017906

Acquiring Editor: Matt Davis   Production Editor: Mark Karmendy
Marketing Manager: Brian Grimm   Editor: Francie Jones
Director of Development: Kathleen Dolan Davies   Editorial Assistant: Michael Zelenko
Developmental Editor: Susan Rachmeler   Manufacturing Supervisor: Becky Morgan

Printed in the United States of America

CONTENTS

5 COMMUNICATING AND INFLUENCING   97

Chapter Five Activities

6 MOTIVATING AND ENGAGING   141

Chapter Six Activities

7 DEVELOPING AND MANAGING   171

Chapter Seven Activities

ABOUT THE AUTHOR

Karen Lawson is an international consultant, speaker, and author. As founder and president of Lawson Consulting Group, Inc., she has built a successful consulting firm specializing in organization and management development as well as executive coaching. She has extensive consulting and seminar experience in the areas of team development, communication, leadership, and quality service across a wide range of industries. Clients include a variety of prominent organizations from the financial services, pharmaceutical, telecommunications, manufacturing, health care, government, and education sectors. In her consulting work with Fortune 500 companies as well as small businesses, she uses her experience and knowledge of human interaction to help leaders at all levels make a difference in their organizations.

Karen is the author of *The Trainer's Handbook, Updated Edition; The Art of Influencing; Improving On-the-Job Training and Coaching; Improving Performance Through Coaching; The Trainer's Handbook; Train-the-Trainer Facilitator's Guide; Involving Your Audience—Making It Active; Skill Builders: 50 Communication Activities; New Employee Orientation Training;* and *Leadership Development Basics,* and coauthor of *101 Ways to Make Training Active.* She has also written chapters for many edited collections, in addition to numerous articles in professional journals.

She holds a PhD in adult and organizational development from Temple University; an MA in English from the University of Akron; and a BA from Mount Union College. She is also a graduate of the National School of Banking in Fairfield, Connecticut. She is one of only four hundred people worldwide to have earned the Certified Speaking Professional designation from the four-thousand-member National Speakers Association. She has received numerous awards for her outstanding contributions to the training and speaking professions, and was named one of Pennsylvania's "Best 50 Women in Business" as well as one of the Philadelphia region's "Women of Distinction."

She has been actively involved in such professional organizations as the National Speakers Association and the American Society for Training and Development, holding leadership positions at both the local and national levels. She is also an active member of the Union League of Philadelphia.

Karen is currently an adjunct professor at Arcadia University in its International MBA program, and she has taught at several colleges and universities at the graduate and undergraduate levels. She has presented at several professional conferences in the United States, Asia, and Europe.

THE TRAINER'S HANDBOOK OF LEADERSHIP DEVELOPMENT

CHAPTER ONE

INTRODUCTION

In this fast-paced global environment of the twenty-first century, the need for effective leaders has never been greater. There is no doubt we are experiencing a leadership deficit throughout our society—in corporations, governments, and communities. Almost daily we are bombarded by articles in newspapers, professional publications, blogs, and other various media bemoaning the lack of qualified leaders to meet the challenges of a diverse workforce, global competition, and an uncertain economy. As a result, organizations are experiencing increased pressure to develop their leaders from within.

The first step in leadership development is to identify organization-specific leadership competencies and characteristics. The next step is to equip the organization's leaders with the behaviors, knowledge, and skills to meet the needs and expectations of their employees, customers, communities, and other stakeholders. The biggest challenge you may face in developing leaders is to create learning experiences and tools that enable the organization's potential and current leaders to internalize and demonstrate necessary leadership traits and behaviors that will ensure the organization's success.

PURPOSE

This activity-based book is designed to provide leaders and those responsible for training leaders with a variety of tools and techniques for developing leadership competencies and characteristics. In addition to emphasizing basic core management skills, this work is influenced by current research on leadership practices and addresses less "tangible" characteristics and traits, such as empathy, agility, authenticity, resilience, and congruence, just to name a few.

The book draws on research by such thought leaders as Warren Bennis, Ken Blanchard, James Kouzes, and Barry Posner, as well as organizations including the Society for Human Resource Management, the Corporate Leadership Council, the Center for Creative Leadership, Right Management Consultants, and others.

INTENDED AUDIENCE

This is a "must have" for busy professionals who are charged with developing leadership competencies and characteristics. Readers who will benefit from this book include

- Chief learning officers and other learning leaders
- Organization development professionals
- Human resource professionals
- Senior managers and other leaders
- Consultants

The book presents a practical, easy-to-use leadership development toolkit that is readily adaptable for both group and individual application. It includes thought-provoking activities designed to create real behavior change. Several of the activities can be used for self-study as part of a structured leadership development program. The book also provides resources and methods for addressing "difficult-to-teach" leadership traits.

HOW THIS BOOK IS ORGANIZED

The Trainer's Handbook of Leadership Development reflects the active-training techniques described in *The Trainer's Handbook, Updated Edition* (Lawson, 2009). The activities are based on adult learning theory, follow the experiential learning cycle, and address all three learning domains: cognitive, affective, and behavioral. Incorporated in the activities are self-assessments, checklists, models, and other valuable handouts and resources.

Chapter Two identifies the forty-five leadership competencies and characteristics addressed in the activities. Each competency or characteristic includes a definition, one or more relevant quotations, and a brief description of the importance of that skill or trait to leadership effectiveness. You can use this information to enhance the process and discussion described for each activity.

Chapter Three helps you begin a leadership development seminar or workshop series by providing four activities to help create the context and prompt participants to begin thinking about and exploring the concept of effective leadership. You may elect to use any or all four of the activities—and in any order—depending on the intent and the time available for the introductory portion of the training design. You can use the two matrices in Chapter Three to determine the activities you want to use to address a particular competency or characteristic.

Chapters Four through Eight are the heart of the book. These chapters include all the activities related to the leadership competencies and characteristics described in Chapter Two. Each activity is arranged as follows:

- Identification of the competency or competencies addressed in the activity
- Brief description of the activity
- The activity's goal or goals—that is, what participants will be able to do as a result of experiencing the activity
- Amount of time required
- Materials and preparation
- Step-by-step process for introducing and conducting the activity
- Suggested discussion questions to debrief the activity
- One or more suggested variations for modifying the activity
- Accompanying handouts, such as checklists, assessments, models, case studies, role-play instructions, and so on

You can use the activities to design a leadership development program "from scratch," or as enhancements to existing modules. However you choose to use them, you will find them to be engaging, energizing, enlightening ways to involve, inspire, and influence the participants in your leadership development programs.

CHAPTER TWO

LEADERSHIP COMPETENCIES AND CHARACTERISTICS

The line between leadership competencies and characteristics is sometimes blurred. People often disagree as to the definitions of the terms. For our purposes, *characteristics* refer, on the one hand, to attributes, traits, or distinguishing qualities. On the other hand, *competencies* are behaviors, skills, or knowledge identified as performance standards for a particular job or responsibility. Taken together, characteristics and competencies create a set of behaviors critical to leadership success. Although there is a distinction between the two terms, we will be using them interchangeably to avoid confusion.

This chapter identifies leadership competencies and characteristics essential for leadership success. It also provides the definition, a relevant quotation or quotations, and a brief discussion of the importance or significance of each attribute.

Although the competencies and characteristics identified in this chapter are based on current popular research (including surveys and studies), the list is by no means exhaustive. By the same token, you should not try to address all of them. Begin by identifying the required and desired leadership competencies and characteristics specific to your organization—or those that would have universal application.

As you review the list and the definitions, please note that many are interrelated. For example, ethics relates to trust and congruence. Communicating can incorporate listening, observing, and giving feedback. For the purpose of designing your topical modules, you may choose to select activities that you can "cluster."

Accountability

Definition: The willingness to follow through on commitments and accept responsibility for one's own actions and decisions.

Quotation: "You must take personal responsibility. You cannot change the circumstances, the seasons, or the wind, but you can change yourself." *Jim Rohn*

Importance: Placing blame, pointing fingers, and complaining about others have no place in leadership. People expect their leaders to take ownership of decisions, policies, and actions. Real leaders take charge of a problem and start working toward a solution instead of finding someone or something to blame. When leaders create a culture of individual and organizational accountability, overall performance improves.

Adaptability/Flexibility/Agility

Definition: The ability to adjust quickly and easily to different conditions, and to adapt to rapidly changing conditions, challenging circumstances, and external pressures.

Quotation: "The pessimist complains about the wind. The optimist expects it to change. The leader adjusts the sails." *William Arthur Ward*

Importance: In today's rapidly changing environment, leaders must be able to "adjust the sails" on a moment's notice or be left behind. They have to be able to adapt their attitudes and behaviors to work effectively with different people and situations.

Authenticity

Definition: The demonstration of genuineness; the quality of being real, not "phony."

Quotation: "Nothing is more effective than sincere, concrete praise, and nothing is more lame than a cookie-cutter compliment." *Bill Walsh, NFL coach*

Importance: We've all heard that actions speak louder than words. This is particularly true as it applies to leadership. People are more likely to believe what you do rather than what you say. When you say one thing and do something else, you risk alienating followers, colleagues, and customers. It is important to demonstrate consistent, congruent behavior on a daily basis.

Balancing Personal and Professional

Definition: Properly prioritizing between career and job responsibilities and other parts of your life (for example, family, leisure, pleasure, spirituality, and so on), resulting in a sense of enjoyment and achievement.

Quotation: "Just as your car runs more smoothly and requires less energy to go faster and farther when the wheels are in perfect alignment, you perform better when your thoughts, feelings, emotions, goals, and values are in balance." *Brian Tracy*

Importance: The lack of a healthy work-life balance can have a serious, negative impact on a leader's effectiveness and sustainability. A true leader understands that a work-life balance does not mean an equal balance. On the one hand, circumstances will cause your work-life balance to vary. On the other hand, your value system should be the compass that helps you determine the right balance at any given time. The example you set is critical because people will assume what you do is what you value, and they will emulate your behavior.

Clarifying Expectations

Definition: Communicating clearly what we expect, including standards of performance; communicating our faith that the individual will meet or exceed those expectations.

Quotations: "If we treat people as though they are what they should be, we help them become what they are capable of becoming." *Johann Wolfgang von Goethe*

"High expectations are the key to everything." *Sam Walton*

Importance: The power of expectation alone can influence the behavior of others. When we communicate to others our high expectations of them, their self-confidence will grow, their capabilities will develop, and their accomplishments will be many. A manager's high expectations lead to high productivity, and low expectations result in low productivity. Studies show that when leaders create a supportive, nurturing culture, people do what they believe is expected of them.

Clarifying Values

Definition: Discovering one's own and others' values by assessing, exploring, and determining what those values are and how they affect personal decision making and behavior.

Quotation: "Nothing can bring you peace but yourself. Nothing can bring you peace but the triumph of principles." *Ralph Waldo Emerson*

Importance: Values are the collective set of deeply ingrained beliefs, ethics, principles, and priorities that guide organizational and individual behavior. Our values provide the basis for our decisions and actions. Values help us set priorities, and they influence the choices and decisions we make every day.

It is important to understand our own values and become more aware of the values of others. Understanding our own value system can help us work and live more effectively in today's world. Many problems of communication, productivity, and interpersonal relations, and their resulting conflicts, lie primarily in significantly different value systems. If we can better understand what motivates others' behavior as well as our own, we can improve our personal and professional relationships.

Coaching

Definition: Giving feedback and support to employees to overcome a performance problem or to gain greater competence; encouraging people to do more than they ever imagined they could.

Quotation: "I never cease to be amazed at the power of the coaching process to draw out the skills or talent that was previously hidden within an individual, and which invariably finds a way to solve a problem previously thought unsolvable." *John Russell*

Importance: Coaching is one of the most critical skills to be mastered by today's leader. Why is coaching so important? Today's environment has created more pressure to do more with less. The key to reducing pressure and get better results is to make the most of an organization's most valuable resource—people.

Successful coaches in business, as in sports, are great influencers. They know how to bring out the best in others. They also know that coaching is an ongoing process and a primary responsibility.

Communicating

Definition: Delivering your message with clarity so that the receiver of your message understands exactly what you want or what you want to convey; soliciting input from others.

Quotation: "If you just communicate you can get by. But if you skillfully communicate, you can work miracles." *Jim Rohn*

Importance: The ability to create an atmosphere of trust and openness that will improve all channels of communication throughout the organization is critical to a leader's success. The effective leader will actively solicit and listen to input from employees and customers as well as openly share information.

Confidence

Definition: The self-assurance and faith that you will act in a right, proper, or effective way.

Quotation: "Belief in oneself is one of the most important bricks in building any successful venture." *Lydia Child*

Importance: If you don't have confidence in yourself, how can you expect others to have confidence in you? True leaders are successful because they are confident in their abilities. They believe that they are capable, and they trust their own judgment. They also project confidence by making decisions, following through, seeking advice from others when appropriate, and not being afraid to admit mistakes.

Congruence

Definition: The demonstration of behavior that is in alignment with one's own values and beliefs; the state of consistency between word and deed—that is, "walking the talk."

Quotation: "People may doubt what you say, but they will believe what you do." *Lewis Cass, American military officer and politician*

Importance: Congruence is related directly to authenticity. Effective leaders are clear about their values, and their behavior is consistent with those values; they do not compromise those values in order to get ahead.

Courage

Definition: The ability to use mental or moral strength to face difficulty without fear.

Quotation: "Courage is the most important of all the virtues because without courage you can't practice any other virtue with consistency." *Maya Angelou*

Importance: A true leader is willing to stand up for what he or she believes, make tough decisions, and take risks. It takes courage to do the right thing, not just that which is easier or more popular. An effective leader will not follow the path of least resistance, but rather will use the power of integrity and conviction to stay the course in spite of barriers, setbacks, and challenges. When leaders display courage, people are more willing to trust them and follow them.

Cross-Cultural Awareness and Sensitivity

Definition: The ability to interact effectively with people from different cultural backgrounds; cultural intelligence.

Quotation: "Each individual must acknowledge not only otherness in all its forms but also the plurality of his or her own identity, within societies that are themselves plural. Only in this way can cultural diversity be preserved as an adaptive process and as a capacity for expression, creation and innovation." *Koichiro Matsuura, UNESCO director-general*

Importance: In our rapidly globalizing world, the effective leader must have an appreciation for and sensitivity to other cultures. Cultural intelligence involves one's ability to interact effectively with people from other cultures and adapt to situations involving different cultural backgrounds. Heightened cultural awareness and sensitivity will enhance a leader's personal effectiveness and provide a competitive edge in multicultural and global contexts.

Decision Making

Definition: Being able and willing to make sound and appropriate choices among available options.

Quotation: "Be willing to make decisions. That's the most important quality in a good leader. Don't fall victim to what I call the ready-aim-aim-aim-aim syndrome. You must be willing to fire." *T. Boone Pickens*

Importance: Like it or not, a leader's ability to make decisions is a critical part of his or her responsibility. Effective leaders draw on their critical thinking skills and use a systematic process to make informed decisions. They also know when it is appropriate to ask others for input or allow others to make decisions themselves. Leaders who stall, seem unable to make a decision, procrastinate, or second-guess themselves are not respected or regarded as leaders.

Delegating

Definition: Willingly giving people the responsibility and authority to do something that is normally part of your job as a manager, and then holding them accountable for their performance.

Quotation: "No man will make a great leader who wants to do it all himself or get all the credit for doing it." *Andrew Carnegie*

Importance: Managers frequently complain that they have too much to do and too little time in which to do it. Unchecked, this feeling leads to stress and managerial ineffectiveness. The inability to delegate frequently has led to the downfall of many leaders—from presidents to first-line supervisors. Mastering the art of delegation makes a leader more effective and provides a means to develop employees.

Empathy

Definition: The ability to identify with the feelings, thoughts, or attitudes of others and to communicate that awareness and understanding.

Quotations: "You can never understand someone unless you understand their point-of-view, climb in that person's skin or stand and walk in that person's shoes." *Atticus Finch, character in Harper Lee's* To Kill a Mockingbird

"If there is any one secret of success, it lies in the ability to get the other's point of view and see things from his angle as well as your own." *Henry Ford*

Importance: The ability to look beyond ourselves into the hearts and souls of others and to identify the common bond of humanity is what empathy is all about. Empathy helps us to identify with the things and people around us—to recognize ourselves in others, and others in us. Empathy skills are critical to your success as a leader because empathy is the foundation of the helping process. Leaders who demonstrate more empathy have better relationships with their employees and are viewed as better performers by their bosses.

Empowering

Definition: Enabling others to think, behave, take action, and control their work and decision making.

Quotation: "Never tell people how to do things. Tell them what to do and they will surprise you with their ingenuity." *George S. Patton*

Importance: Fostering empowerment means making people feel valued by involving them in decisions, incorporating their ideas, asking them to participate in the planning process, praising them, and recognizing and rewarding them for their achievements and efforts. Empowered employees are engaged employees, and engaged employees are more committed and involved in their organization and less likely to leave.

Enthusiasm and Passion

Definition: The excitement, exuberance, and enjoyment you have for whatever you are involved in.

Quotations: "Enthusiasm is one of the most powerful engines of success. When you do a thing, do it with all your might. Put your whole soul into it. Stamp it with your own personality. Be active, be energetic and faithful, and you will accomplish your objective. Nothing great was ever achieved without enthusiasm." *Ralph Waldo Emerson*

"Enthusiasm spells the difference between mediocrity and accomplishment." *Norman Vincent Peale*

Importance: Passion and enthusiasm are contagious. People who are passionate about what they do and believe in can have a tremendous influence on others. When you are excited or enthusiastic about a cause, task, or project, that enthusiasm spreads to others. As a leader, you can't ignite a fire in others unless there is first one burning inside you.

Ethics

Definition: The standards of conduct that guide our behavior; a set of high moral principles and behaviors.

Quotation: "Ethical behavior is related to self-esteem. . . . [P]eople who feel good about themselves have what it takes to withstand outside pressure and to do what is right rather than do what is merely expedient, popular, or lucrative. . . . [A] strong code or morality in any business is the first step toward its success." *Ken Blanchard and Norman Vincent Peale*

Importance: Ethics are based on our value system and define who we are; ethics are what we do. Values help us set priorities; ethics set boundaries for behavior. Thus, ethics are value-driven, behavior-oriented, and situational.

Fairness

Definition: The just and honest treatment of employees, free from bias and prejudice.

Quotation: "Fairness is not an attitude. It's a professional skill that must be developed and exercised." *Brit Hume*

Importance: When people feel they are receiving fair and equitable treatment, they are not only happier in their job but also more likely to trust their leaders, and eager to meet expectations. Effective leaders create a positive work environment characterized by fair and equitable job assignments, reward and recognition systems, and criteria for promoting qualified people.

Focus

Definition: The concentration of effort or attention.

Quotation: "Concentrate all your thoughts upon the work at hand. The sun's rays do not burn until brought to a focus." *Alexander Graham Bell*

Importance: An effective leader maintains focus by concentrating on what is important. Importance is directly related to vision, mission, goals, and values. Clear focus enables the leader to stay on course through turbulent times.

Giving Feedback

Definition: Describing for others our perceptions of and reaction to their actions; giving information to others about their behavior.

Quotation: "Not everything that is faced can be changed, but nothing can be changed until it is faced." *James Baldwin*

Importance: The purpose of feedback is not to tear down; it must be constructive, not destructive, intended to inform and enlighten, and delivered with genuine care and concern. Feedback is fundamental to developing and maintaining relationships. Feedback lets a person know how his or her behavior feels to another and how it affects the other person. When we deliver feedback in the form of "I messages," the receiver generally recognizes it as a positive attempt to communicate our needs, wants, and concerns. As a result, the receiver is much more likely to respond positively rather than becoming defensive, combative, or uncooperative.

Goal Setting

Definition: Making a statement of outcome and specific accountability that you seek to achieve over a specified period of time; striving to attain a goal that meets the following criteria:

Specific: What task will be accomplished if the goal is achieved?

Measurable: What are the performance standards?

Attainable/Achievable: Do you have the ability to do it?

Realistic: Can it be done?

Time-bound: When is this goal to be achieved?

Quotations: "From nowhere a Cheshire cat appeared in the tree and asked Alice, 'Can I help you?'

"Alice said, 'Yes, please. I'm lost and need to know which road I should take.'

"The Cheshire cat asked, 'Where are you going?'

"Alice said, 'I don't know!'

"'Well,' said the Cheshire cat, 'then it doesn't matter which road you take.'"

Lewis Carroll, Alice in Wonderland

"Long-range goals keep you from being frustrated by short-term failures."

James Cash Penney

Importance: Setting goals is the first step to achieving excellence—both personally and professionally. Goals are ways to measure results and assess success. Ill-defined goals lead people in different directions. As a leader, it is critical to establish a shared understanding of what the individual or group is to accomplish. When a goal does not specify desired results, people will define their own results. People need to know what is expected of them and have some way to measure how well they are doing relative to the target.

Humor

Definition: The ability to perceive, enjoy, or express what is amusing; the ability to laugh at yourself and not take yourself so seriously.

Quotation: "A sense of humor is part of the art of leadership, of getting along with people, of getting things done." *Dwight D. Eisenhower*

Importance: A sense of humor is an important characteristic of an effective leader. A manager who demonstrates a good sense of humor creates an open and relaxed work environment in which people can flourish.

Influencing

Definition: Being a compelling force on the thoughts, opinions, behaviors, and attitudes of others.

Quotation: "Think twice before you speak, because your words and influence will plant the seed of either success or failure in the mind of another." *Napoleon Hill*

Importance: In today's world, lines of authority are blurred as people work cross-functionally in teams. Structurally flat organizations require people to manage processes and projects that involve people over whom they have no formal authority. As a result, leaders must rely more on their ability to influence in order to get things done. People who have little power are capable of exercising tremendous influence on people with whom they interact, regardless of position. The truly powerful individual is one who relates to and interacts well with people at all levels.

Innovation/Creativity

Definition: The ability and willingness to introduce new ideas and ways of doing things (implies changes in thinking, products, processes, or organizations; requires being forward-looking and ahead of current thinking).

Quotations: "Innovation distinguishes between a leader and a follower." *Steve Jobs*

"Nothing is more dangerous than an idea when it is the only one you have." *Emile Chartier*

Importance: In today's complex, corporate environment, leaders face significant challenges. Globalization, technology, changing demographics, and outsourcing create pressure for constant innovation. New approaches to work, productivity, and people management require leaders at all levels to engage in "out-of-the-box" thinking and implement groundbreaking business strategies and tactics.

Judgment

Definition: The ability to distinguish among, evaluate, or assess situations, draw sound conclusions, and act accordingly.

Quotation: "With good judgment, little else matters; without it, nothing else matters." *Noel Tichy*

Importance: Leaders in government, business, sports, and the military are remembered for their best and worst judgment calls. The quality of a leader's judgment determines the success or failure of the organization.

Leading Change

Definition: Being able to transition individuals and organizations from a current state to a desired future state.

Quotation: "Only in growth, reform, and change, paradoxically enough, is true security to be found." *Anne Morrow Lindbergh*

Importance: The leader is the key to change. The leader's own attitudes and the way he or she approaches change are critical. How managers implement change is the determining factor in the more successful transitions and transformations.

In a sea of uncertainty, managers themselves can display either positive or negative behaviors. Unproductive behaviors fall into the categories of *hide* ("I'm pretending the problem will go away"), *wait and see* ("This could be another passing fad"), or *blame* ("Senior management is creating this chaos, and there is nothing I can do about it"). Conversely, productive behaviors involve (1) helping employees deal with change and (2) acting as a change agent within an organization. As a change agent, the leader is often expected to facilitate a specific change easily and effectively, with a minimum of disruption and with maximum support from the group.

Listening

Definition: In a two-way process, taking in information from the sender or speaker without judging, clarifying what we think we heard, and responding to the speaker in a way that invites the communication to continue.

Quotation: "Seek first to understand, then to be understood." *Stephen Covey*

Importance: Studies show that we spend 80 percent of our waking hours communicating, and according to research at least 45 percent of that time is spent listening. Although listening is a primary activity, most individuals are inefficient listeners. By listening, leaders will discover what motivates their employees to do a good job and their clients to buy a product or service. Listening is the catalyst that fosters mutual understanding and provides us with insight into people's needs and desires so that we can connect with them.

Managing Conflict

Definition: Identifying and handling conflict within the organization.

Quotation: "A good manager doesn't try to eliminate conflict; he tries to keep it from wasting the energies of his people." *Robert Townsend*

Importance: Our ability to manage conflict when interacting with others in our work environment is becoming increasingly important. Conflict is defined as a situation in which someone believes his or her needs have been denied. In today's workplaces, situations in which someone believes his or her needs have been denied occur every day. The resulting conflict makes it imperative that we master effective conflict management skills. These skills are needed not only when we are involved personally in conflict situations but also to manage conflict within the teams or groups we work with daily.

Managing Performance

Definition: Setting clear, realistic expectations, communicating those expectations, monitoring performance, and measuring individual performance on an ongoing basis.

Quotation: "It is an immutable law in business that words are words, explanations are explanations, promises are promises—but only performance is reality." *Harold S. Geneen*

Importance: Performance management is one of the most important responsibilities of a leader. It is also the most time consuming because it involves setting and clearly communicating specific expectations, monitoring performance without micromanaging, providing ongoing feedback both positive and negative, and coaching as needed to improve performance.

Mentoring

Definition: Fostering a personal development relationship in which you as the more experienced or more knowledgeable person help a less experienced or less knowledgeable person.

Quotation: "We make a living by what we get, we make a life by what we give."
Winston Churchill

Importance: Leading organizations today recognize the importance of the mentoring relationship. In fact, many have established a formal mentoring program. Mentoring is an effective way of developing an organization's intellectual capital to remain competitive. It is also effective in retaining top talent. Mutual trust, respect, and communication are important elements in the mentoring relationship.

Motivating

Definition: Creating an environment in which employees feel they are making a real contribution and are eager to come to work and perform at peak capacity.

Quotations: "Knowing what people need and want is the key to understanding them. And if you can understand them, you can influence them and impact their lives in a positive way." *John Maxwell*

"You get the best effort from others not by lighting a fire beneath them, but by building a fire within." *Bob Nelson*

Importance: Today's workplace is a fast-paced and challenging environment. Global competition and rapidly changing technology have resulted in new skill requirements and more complex jobs with fewer qualified people to fill them. Faced with a shrinking talent pool and more "me-focused" employees, companies are finding it increasingly difficult to attract, motivate, and retain top talent. The "old ways" of leading and motivating just don't work anymore. Effective leaders are those who learn how to create an environment in which people thrive and are committed to helping their organization succeed.

Networking

Definition: Developing, maintaining, and leveraging connections with people outside your organization to share information and services, seek advice, and offer mutual support; building a base of influence by developing strong personal and professional relationships.

Quotation: "Build good relationships and profitable transactions will follow."
Philip Kotler

Importance: Successful people are masters of networking. Networking skills help you build a base of influence by developing strong personal and professional relationships. The benefits of networking can be summarized in three simple words: *relationships, opportunities,* and *resources.*

Relationship building results in both personal and professional enrichment. The people you meet and who become part of your network are valuable resources of information about your industry, your profession, other people, and even organizations. They are resources for gaining access to people and a source of referrals and business leads.

Observing

Definition: Becoming aware or taking notice of the world around you; gaining insight.

Quotation: "Perceptive observation is seeing with your brain, feeling with your eyes, interpreting with your heart." *Robert Wade*

Importance: True leaders observe the world around them and the people in that world. They are very perceptive, which enables them to "tune in" to their followers, colleagues, and customers. They are sensitive to the nonverbal as well as the verbal cues, and thus can take appropriate action.

Problem Solving

Definition: Using a variety of approaches and techniques to solve business problems and to help team members develop these critical skills as well.

Quotation: "No problem can be solved until it is reduced to some simple form. The changing of a vague difficulty into a specific, concrete form is a very essential element in thinking." *J. P. Morgan*

Importance: Each and every day, leaders are faced with problems. The most effective leaders have the ability to look at problems as opportunities, and to use a systematic process to define the real problem and arrive at a solution that will produce long-lasting, positive results.

Questioning

Definition: Asking open-ended questions that start with "how" or "what" and are designed to get people to think for themselves and solve their own problems.

Quotation: "Probably my best quality as a coach is that I ask a lot of challenging questions and let the person come up with the answer." *Phil Dixon*

Importance: Asking rather than telling is a major component of leadership success. By asking the right questions, a leader prompts others to find the best solutions for themselves; gain self-confidence; and think and act more critically, analytically, and creatively. Thoughtful questioning also empowers them to challenge assumptions and take ownership of the solutions.

Relationship Building

Definition: Taking action to establish emotional connections with others.

Quotation: "Leaders, wherever they are, lead by virtue of the relationships they're able to build—that people believe them, trust them, and are willing to follow them." *Rosabeth Moss Kanter*

Importance: Businesses are built on relationships. True leaders recognize the importance of building relationships inside and outside the organization and make it a priority. Leaders can no longer rely on power and position to get things done. They now must develop relationships with people at all levels and use their influencing skills to create and maintain a harmonious, meaningful, and mutually satisfying work environment.

Resilience

Definition: The ability to deal effectively with pressure while remaining optimistic and persistent even under adversity; the ability to recover quickly from setbacks.

Quotation: "The strongest oak of the forest is not the one that is protected from the storm and hidden from the sun. It's the one that stands in the open where it is compelled to struggle for its existence against the winds and rains and the scorching sun." *Napoleon Hill*

Importance: If leaders are not resilient, they will not be successful in their roles. Effective leaders demonstrate resilience by dealing with life's everyday pressures, remaining optimistic no matter how bad things get, and recovering quickly from setbacks.

Risk Taking

Definition: Engaging in activities that could have negative results or uncertain outcomes.

Quotation: "The greatest mistake you can make in life is continually fearing that you'll make one." *Elbert Hubbard*

Importance: People vary widely as to their willingness to take risks. Many factors influence a leader's risk-taking capabilities, such as personality, corporate culture, past experience, emotional intelligence, and type of industry. An effective leader knows when it is appropriate to take a risk and how much of a risk to take.

Role Modeling

Definition: Demonstrating behavior that others want to emulate; behaving in such a way that you are looked up to or revered, and others aspire to be like you.

Quotation: "Example is not the main thing in influencing others. It is the only thing."
Albert Schweitzer

Importance: Whether you realize it or not, you are a role model for someone. You may have no idea what lives you touch, positively or negatively, by your behavior. Modeling the behavior you expect from others is a powerful influencer.

Self-Awareness

Definition: The ability to assess regularly and honestly your own strengths and short-comings and seek help from others to assume roles or perform tasks for which you do not have the skills or expertise.

Quotations: "The journey of true success and lasting leadership begins with the inward journey to the soul." *James Arthur Ray*

"Knowing others is intelligence; knowing yourself is true wisdom." *Tao Te Ching*

Importance: Effective leaders are keenly aware of their strengths as well as their shortcomings. Leaders who try to hide their weaknesses actually call attention to them. In so doing, they erode others' confidence and belief in them, and undermine their credibility. Rather than trying to hide their weaknesses, effective leaders acknowledge their areas for improvement and surround themselves with those who can compensate for the skills they may lack. They recognize that they don't have all the answers, admit mistakes, and ask for help. True leaders solicit and listen to feedback from those whom they trust to be open and honest in delivering it.

Storytelling

Definition: Communicating the organization's culture through the telling of events that illustrate its history, values, vision, traditions, rituals, and philosophy; conveying your ideas, points of view, principles, and beliefs as a leader.

Quotations: "Stories are easier to remember—because in many ways, stories are *how* we remember." *Daniel Pink*

"A story is a fact wrapped in an emotion that compels us to take an action that transforms our world." *Bob Dickman and Richard Maxwell,* The Elements of Persuasion

Importance: Throughout history, stories have passed from generation to generation as a means of preserving a group's culture, heritage, history, and tradition. Stories teach a lesson as well as entertain. Stories are at the very heart of who we are as human beings. Stories touch us in a way that no other medium can. They help define who we are and what we believe. Storytelling is a great way to connect with your employees as well as your customers and colleagues.

Team Building

Definition: Working collaboratively with others both inside and outside the organization to achieve organizational goals.

Quotation: "To promote cooperation and teamwork, remember: People tend to resist that which is forced upon them. People tend to support that which they help to create." *Vince Pfaff*

Importance: Effective leaders create a team environment that relies heavily on good communication, cooperation, collaboration, conflict resolution, clarification of roles, consideration, and commitment. In addition, they provide the necessary support, guidance, and positive reinforcement that encourage a true team spirit and net incredible results.

Trust Building

Definition: Fostering others' confidence in and willingness to act on the basis of your words, actions, or decisions, and demonstrating similar confidence in them.

Quotations: "Integrity is the basis of trust, which is not so much an ingredient of leadership as it is a product. It is the one quality that cannot be acquired but must be earned. It is given by coworkers and followers, and without it, the leader can't function." *Warren Bennis*

"Trust is ultimately what allows leaders to lead. . . . If you are not trusted as a leader, people will not truly work to implement your vision or will require so much 'proof' of your direction that your initiatives fall victim to slow or poor execution." *Craig Weatherup*

Importance: Trust is the basis of all human relationships and is an essential element of business success. Developed over time, it involves a commitment to building interpersonal relationships based on honesty, integrity, and a genuine concern for others. Low levels of trust cause high levels of stress, reduce productivity, stifle innovation, and hamper the decision-making process. High levels of trust, conversely, increase employee morale, reduce absenteeism, promote innovation, and aid in managing change effectively. In essence, trust is the result of all the other characteristics and competencies addressed in this book.

From a leadership perspective, trust works two ways. First, effective leaders must demonstrate the behaviors that earn the *trust of* others. Second, such leaders demonstrate *trust in* others. They empower their employees by delegating responsibility, allowing them to make decisions, and giving them opportunities to develop.

Visioning

Definition: Thinking long term; being future-oriented; having a mental picture of what the organization should look like, feel like, and be seen as in the future.

Quotations: "Show me a leader without a vision, and I'll show you someone who isn't going anywhere. At best, he is traveling in circles." *John Maxwell*

"Vision is the art of seeing what is invisible to others." *Jonathan Swift*

"Vision without action is merely a dream. Action without vision just passes the time. Vision with action can change the world." *Joel Barker*

Importance: A vision creates a purpose, helps maintain focus, and inspires and motivates others. It is the glue that binds a group and energizes it. A true leader has a clear vision and communicates it clearly. If we want an organization to be successful, we must first have some idea of what that success will look like, and then tap into our resources—our employees—to help us realize our vision. When employees understand a leader's vision, they are compelled to participate in its realization.

CHAPTER THREE

DESIGNING A LEADERSHIP DEVELOPMENT PROGRAM

Formal training workshops and seminars are the core of any leadership development program. Once the key decision makers have chosen organization-specific leadership competencies and characteristics or you have identified the ones on which you would like to focus, the next steps are to select the right modules or topics to address those skills and traits, and then to determine the appropriate order or sequence of the topics. The program must reflect the organization's management philosophy and desired leadership competencies and practices. Although the specific topics are determined by both individual and organizational needs as identified in the front-end analysis and tied to the strategic plan, the following are suggested core modules:

- Understanding Leadership
  - Definition of leadership
  - Leader versus manager
  - Leadership styles
  - Developing your competencies and characteristics
- Communicating and Influencing
  - Interpersonal skills
  - Communication styles
  - Listening

- Nonverbal communication
- Giving feedback
- Motivating and Engaging Employees
  - Characteristics of today's employees
  - Generational differences
  - What employees value
- Leading Change
  - Managing change
  - Overcoming resistance to change
- Dealing with Conflict
  - Symptoms and causes of conflict
  - Preventing conflict
  - Resolving conflict
- Developing Employees
  - Role of delegating
  - Mentoring
- Managing Performance
  - Setting goals, standards, and expectations
  - Coaching
  - Holding people accountable

These are just a few of the potential competency-based modules of a structured leadership development seminar or workshop series. The length, number, and frequency of the sessions will depend on the program's overall requirements and specifications.

To get you started, this chapter presents four activities you can use in an introductory module that focuses on the concept of leadership and the competencies and characteristics of effective leaders. Also included in this chapter are two charts to help you choose the appropriate activities related to the specific competencies you want to develop.

COMPETENCIES WITH RELATED ACTIVITIES

Competency	Activities
Accountability	Stopping the Blame Game
Adaptability/Flexibility/Agility	Doing It Differently
Authenticity	Being Real
Balancing Personal and Professional	The Balancing Act
Clarifying Expectations	What Do You Expect?
Clarifying Values	Values Collage
Coaching	Applying Your Coaching Skills Describing Behavior
Communicating	Describing Behavior Mixed Messages The Art of Asking Questions What Do You Mean?
Confidence	Distinguishing Behaviors
Congruence	Being Real Living Your Values Mixed Messages Modeling the Way
Courage	Developing Courage
Cross-Cultural Awareness and Sensitivity	Developing Cultural Intelligence
Decision Making	Employee Development Decisions
Delegating	Delegating Effectively Self-Assessment Delegation Case Study Delegation Process
Empathy	What Is It Like?
Empowering	Empowering Others

(Continued)

Competency	Activities
Enthusiasm and Passion	Fired Up!
Ethics	Do the Right Thing
Fairness	Fair or Equal?
Focus	Setting Priorities
Giving Feedback	Describing Behavior Giving Feedback
Goal Setting	On Target
Humor	Make Them Laugh
Influencing	Heroes and Heroines The Art of Influencing
Innovation/Creativity	Innovation or Creativity?
Judgment	Making the Right Call
Leading Change	Embracing Change How to Present Change to Employees Leading Change
Listening	Active Listening Responses Listening Self-Awareness Assessment Mixed Messages
Managing Conflict	Common Ground Conflicting Agendas
Managing Performance	Describing Behavior Performance Management Skills Checklist
Mentoring	The Magic of Mentoring What Mentors Do
Motivating	Showing Appreciation What Do Your Employees Value? What Is It Like?
Networking	Networking Checklist

Competency	Activities
Observing	Active Observation Picture This
Problem Solving	Figure It Out
Questioning	Stopping the Blame Game The Art of Asking Questions
Relationship Building	Things We Have in Common What Is It Like?
Resilience	Bouncing Back
Risk Taking	Risk Attitudes Inventory Permission or Forgiveness?
Role Modeling	Heroes and Heroines Modeling the Way
Self-Awareness	Mirror, Mirror Who Am I?
Storytelling	Tell Me a Story
Team Building	Creating a Team Identity Team Models
Trust Building	Trust Me
Visioning	Into the Future

ACTIVITIES RELATED TO COMPETENCIES

Activity	Competencies
Active Listening Responses	Listening
Active Observation	Observing
Applying Your Coaching Skills	Coaching

(*Continued*)

Activity	Competencies
Being Real	Authenticity Congruence
Bouncing Back	Resilience
Case Study—Employee Development Decisions	Decision Making
Common Ground	Managing Conflict
Conflicting Agendas	Managing Conflict
Creating a Team Identity	Team Building
Delegating Effectively Self-Assessment	Delegating
Delegation Case Study	Delegating
Delegation Process	Delegating
Describing Behavior	Coaching Communicating Giving Feedback Managing Performance
Developing Courage	Courage
Developing Cultural Intelligence	Cross-Cultural Awareness and Sensitivity
Distinguishing Behaviors	Confidence
Do the Right Thing	Ethics
Doing It Differently	Adaptability/Flexibility/Agility
Embracing Change	Leading Change
Empowering Others	Empowering
Fair or Equal?	Fairness
Figure It Out	Problem Solving
Fired Up!	Enthusiasm and Passion
Giving Feedback	Giving Feedback
Heroes and Heroines	Influencing Role Modeling

Activity	Competencies
How to Present Change to Employees	Leading Change
Innovation or Creativity?	Innovation/Creativity
Into the Future	Visioning
Leading Change	Leading Change
Listening Self-Awareness Assessment	Listening
Living Your Values	Congruence
Make Them Laugh	Humor
Making the Right Call	Judgment
Mirror, Mirror	Self-Awareness
Mixed Messages	Communicating Congruence Listening
Modeling the Way	Congruence Role Modeling
Networking Checklist	Networking
On Target	Goal Setting
Performance Management Skills Checklist	Managing Performance
Permission or Forgiveness?	Risk Taking
Picture This	Observing
Risk Attitudes Inventory	Risk Taking
Setting Priorities	Focus
Showing Appreciation	Motivating
Stopping the Blame Game	Accountability Questioning
Team Models	Team Building
Tell Me a Story	Storytelling

(Continued)

Activity	Competencies
The Art of Asking Questions	Communicating Questioning
The Art of Influencing	Influencing
The Balancing Act	Balancing Personal and Professional
The Magic of Mentoring	Mentoring
Things We Have in Common	Relationship Building
Trust Me	Trust Building
Values Collage	Clarifying Values
What Do You Expect?	Clarifying Expectations
What Do You Mean?	Communicating
What Do Your Employees Value?	Motivating
What Is It Like?	Empathy Motivating Relationship Building
What Mentors Do	Mentoring
Who Am I?	Self-Awareness

A CHECKLIST FOR EFFECTIVE LEADERSHIP

Description: This self-assessment activity enables participants to reflect on effective leadership behaviors and how well they practice them.

Goal:

- Identify the leadership behaviors participants would like to improve.

Time Required: 30 minutes

Materials and Preparation:

- *A Checklist for Effective Leadership* (one per participant)

Process:

1. Introduce the activity by explaining that effective leaders are keenly aware of their strengths and their opportunities for improvement.
2. Explain that this activity is designed to give participants an opportunity to assess informally the behaviors they need to improve in order to be more effective as leaders.
3. Distribute *A Checklist for Effective Leadership* and ask them to put a check mark next to each behavior they wish to improve. Give them 8 minutes.
4. At the end of the 8 minutes, reconvene the entire group and ask them to work in pairs to share the areas on which they would like to improve. Give them 10 minutes.
5. At the end of the 10 minutes, reconvene the group and ask volunteers to share specific behaviors they would like to improve.

Discussion:

1. What was your reaction to completing the checklist?
2. What did you learn about yourself?
3. How can you use this checklist to help you become a more effective leader?

Variations:

- Instead of asking participants to respond to this checklist during the session, you could instead have them complete it as "homework" and bring it to the next session.
- You may choose to use a specific leadership assessment rather than this checklist.

EFFECTIVE LEADERSHIP CHECKLIST

Use the following as a checklist for improving your leadership skills. Put a check mark next to those you wish to improve.

☐ 1. Be a role model by "practicing what you preach."

☐ 2. Demand excellence by setting and communicating performance standards and holding people accountable.

☐ 3. Use coaching skills to help others improve performance or further develop their capabilities.

☐ 4. Give immediate and relevant feedback on an ongoing basis.

☐ 5. Develop people by training, cross-training, and providing growth opportunities.

☐ 6. Explain to others how their job and tasks relate to organizational goals.

☐ 7. Empower people to make decisions, particularly when those decisions affect them in some way.

☐ 8. Lead by influence, not power and authority.

☐ 9. Respect others and maintain every individual's dignity at all times.

☐ 10. Use rewards, praise, and positive reinforcement.

☐ 11. Admit and apologize when you are wrong.

☐ 12. Solicit feedback from others about your behavior and performance.

☐ 13. Communicate openly and honestly with others on a regular basis.

☐ 14. Encourage others to ask for support and assistance.

☐ 15. Listen to and deal effectively with others' concerns and complaints.

☐ 16. Tailor motivational techniques to meet the needs of the individual.

☐ 17. Link rewards to specific behaviors and performance.

NATURE OR NURTURE?

Description: In this point-counterpoint activity, participants explore the concept of leadership as something that can be developed.

Goal:
- Examine participants' attitudes toward the ability to develop leaders.

Time Required: 15 minutes

Materials and Preparation:
- Slide or flip chart page on which the following appears: "Leaders are born, not made."

Process:
1. Introduce the activity by explaining that participants will have an opportunity to explore the concept of leadership through a point-counterpoint exercise.
2. Display the following statement on a flip chart page or slide: "Leaders are born, not made."
3. Divide the group into two subgroups.
4. Ask one subgroup to discuss and come up with points in support of the statement.
5. Ask the other subgroup to prepare arguments against the statement.
6. Give the subgroups 3 minutes to prepare their arguments or key points.
7. At the end of the 3 minutes, call time. Begin the discussion by asking a person from the subgroup in support of the statement to offer one key point. Then ask that person to call on someone in the other subgroup to offer a counterpoint.
8. Continue this back-and-forth, "call-on-the-next-speaker" format for 3 minutes. At the end of the 3 minutes, lead a discussion about what participants learned about their (and others') attitudes toward the concept of leadership.

Discussion:
1. What was your reaction to the activity?
2. How did you feel if you had to take a position with which you did not agree?
3. What was your reaction when you heard some of the arguments from the other side?
4. What insights did you gain about the concept of leadership?
5. What is the difference between "nature" and "nurture"?

Variation:
- Rather than conducting a point-counterpoint discussion, you could put people in small groups to discuss the meaning of the statement and give specific examples from their own experience.

TRAITS OF EFFECTIVE LEADERS

Description: This small-group activity introduces participants to the concept of leadership and what competencies and characteristics leaders need to be effective.

Goals:
- Explain the difference between a manager and a leader.
- Identify competencies and characteristics of effective leaders.

Time Required: 30 minutes

Materials and Preparation:
- List of key competencies and characteristics
- Flip chart pages
- Markers
- Masking tape

Process:
1. Introduce the activity by asking the following questions:
   - How many of you think you are a good manager?
   - How many of you think you are a good leader?
   - Would you rather be known as a good manager or a good leader? Why?
2. Explain that you are going to give them an opportunity to explore the difference between a manager and a leader, and the characteristics, skills, qualities, and traits of effective leaders.
3. Divide the group into subgroups of five to seven people.
4. Give each subgroup two flip chart pages and a marker.
5. Explain that the activity has two parts:
   - First, they are to identify three famous people they would label as *effective* leaders. Explain that these people can be real or fictional, alive or dead. Emphasize that they should choose people everyone would recognize.
   - Second, after they have identified the three people, they should compile one list of leadership characteristics, skills, qualities, and traits that would apply to all three people they chose. Point out that each subgroup is developing one list only, not one list per person.
6. Ask them to put their lists on the flip chart pages and tell them they have 8 minutes to complete the task.

7. At the end of the time period, ask them to post their lists on the walls around the room.

8. Ask them to review each subgroup's selection of three leaders and invite the participants to challenge names or ask for further clarification as to the reason a subgroup selected a particular individual.

9. Next, ask the group to identify common traits and skills found on the lists. Note them by circling the words or phrases on the subgroups' lists.

10. Compare the group-generated list with a list of characteristics and competencies you have chosen to emphasize in the program.

Discussion:

1. What was your reaction to the activity?
2. What is the difference between a leader and a manager?
3. What is significant about the word *effective?*
4. How do you think you "measure up" to the list?

Variation:

- Instead of asking the subgroups each to generate a list of the characteristics, skills, qualities, and traits of an effective leader, you could provide them with your selected list and ask them to give examples of leaders who have demonstrated those particular attributes.

WORDS TO LEAD BY

Description: This activity introduces participants to leadership competencies and characteristics through the thoughts and perspectives of others who study and practice effective leadership.

Goal:

• Explore various perspectives on what it takes to be an effective leader.

Time Required: 20 minutes

Materials and Preparation:

• Select several quotations from Chapter Two that relate to the competencies you are going to address in your program.
• Print each quotation on a flip chart page and post these on the walls around the room.

Process:

1. Introduce the activity by explaining that you want to get participants thinking about the various competencies and characteristics of effective leaders.
2. Divide the group into subgroups of four or five people.
3. Assign each subgroup a specific quotation, and ask the subgroups to get up and go to where the quotation is posted.
4. Give subgroups 6 to 8 minutes to discuss the meaning of the quotation as it relates to a leadership competency or characteristic, and to give examples of how they have demonstrated that behavior or have observed someone else who demonstrated that behavior.
5. At the end of the designated time period, ask a representative from each subgroup to summarize their discussion for the rest of the group.

Discussion:

1. How relevant are the quotations to you as a leader?
2. Which one of the quotations did you find particularly inspiring?
3. What did you learn from the activity?
4. How can these "words of wisdom" help you in your leadership role?

Variations:

• Rather than use the quotations from Chapter Two, you can select quotations from your own sources.
• Instead of assigning subgroups to specific quotations, subgroups can "sign up" for their favorite quotation by moving to the place in the room where their choice is posted.

CHAPTER FOUR

INCREASING AWARENESS–SELF AND OTHERS

Effective leaders have a keen sense of awareness of both themselves and others. They know their strengths and shortcomings. They also know what they value, and they practice behaviors that serve as models for others to follow. This chapter includes activities that help leaders become more self-aware. These activities address such intangible leadership qualities such as empathy, courage, risk taking, and passion.

BEING REAL

Competencies: Authenticity, Congruence

Description: This activity allows participants to explore the concept of authenticity as it relates to leadership, and helps them understand how seemingly insignificant behavior can have an impact on how sincere or "real" the leader is perceived to be.

Goals:

- Recognize how tone and inflection can support or contradict a person's intended sincerity.
- Examine the relationship between authentic behavior and effective leadership.

Time Required: 20 minutes

Materials and Preparation:

- *It's How You Say It Activity Sheet* (one per participant)

Process:

1. Introduce the activity by asking participants for examples of "phony," insincere behavior. Ask them what their reaction is to that type of behavior.
2. Explain that true leaders are "real" or genuine when they give praise or compliment someone. Point out that although a person may intend to be sincere, the way in which he or she delivers the message may have the opposite effect.
3. Divide the group into subgroups of six and distribute the *It's How You Say It Activity Sheet.*
4. Ask the participants to take turns delivering the statements on the handout to the members of their subgroup, emphasizing the word that appears in bold.
5. Reconvene the entire group and conduct a general discussion. Ask for volunteers to summarize the meaning of each sentence.

Discussion:

1. What was your reaction to the different ways the sentence was delivered?
2. What changed the meaning of each sentence?
3. Which sentence seemed the most sincere, and why?
4. What did you learn from this activity?
5. If a leader is not perceived as authentic or sincere, how does that affect his or her effectiveness?
6. How does the activity relate to the way you deliver compliments or give positive feedback?

Variation:

- You may choose to read each sentence and have the participants write down their reaction to or interpretation of that statement.

IT'S HOW YOU SAY IT ACTIVITY SHEET

Take turns delivering the statements on the handout to the members of your subgroup, emphasizing the word that appears in bold.

1. **You** did a great job on this project.

2. You **did** a great job on this project.

3. You did a **great** job on this project.

4. You did a great **job** on this project.

5. You did a great job on **this** project.

6. You did a great job on this **project.**

DEVELOPING COURAGE

Competency: Courage

Description: This is an individual writing activity that can help participants explore the concept of courage as a leadership characteristic.

Goals:

- Explain the difference between courage and bravery.
- Identify situations that would require a leader to be courageous.
- Identify ways a person can develop courage.

Time Required: 40 minutes

Materials and Preparation:

- *Developing Courage Worksheet* (one per participant)

Process:

1. Introduce the activity by explaining that courage is one of the fundamental requirements for leaders in any field. Mention that Aristotle said, "Courage is the first of human qualities because it is the quality which guarantees the others." Ask them why they think courage is an important leadership characteristic.

2. Ask them to work in pairs to develop a definition of courage. Give them 3 minutes.

3. After 3 minutes, solicit responses from the group. Point out that courage implies mental or moral strength in spite of fear. The more you confront the fear, the more it diminishes. Courage differs from bravery, which implies a physical deed, such as saving someone from drowning.

4. Mention that courage can be developed and, as actress Ruth Gordon once said, that "courage is very important. Like a muscle, it is strengthened by use."

5. Explain that you are going to give them an opportunity to reflect on their own courageous experiences. Distribute the *Developing Courage Worksheet* and ask them to think about a time when they were courageous. Possible examples are as follows:
   - Showing courage of conviction (speaking out for something you believe)
   - Revealing vulnerability (admitting you don't know something)
   - Dissenting (voicing an unpopular opinion)
   - Overcoming a fear or phobia (conquering a fear of water, flying, public speaking, or making sales calls, for example)

6. Ask them to complete the worksheet individually. Give them 10 minutes.

7. At the end of the 10 minutes, ask them to form pairs and discuss each other's examples of courage.

8. Reconvene the group and ask for volunteers to share their examples.

9. Ask the group for ideas of how people can develop courage. Offer the following suggestions:

   • Acknowledge the fear—that is, admit to yourself that you are afraid.

   • Analyze the fear. What is its basis?

   • Think about a time when you demonstrated courage and how you felt afterward.

   • Visualize yourself overcoming the fear.

   • Confront your fears and take action.

   • Do the thing you fear over and over.

Discussion:

1. How did you feel as you were sharing your example?

2. What did you learn about developing courage?

3. What can you do going forward to help you be more courageous?

Variation:

• This can be used as an individual activity.

DEVELOPING COURAGE WORKSHEET

Think of a time when you were courageous, and then answer the following questions:

1. What was the situation?

2. What prompted you to take action?

3. How did you feel when you were about to confront the issue or take action?

4. How did you feel afterward?

5. What obstacle or challenge do you still want to confront or overcome?

6. How can others help or support you?

DEVELOPING CULTURAL INTELLIGENCE

Competency: Cross-Cultural Awareness and Sensitivity

Description: In this activity, participants explore the various stages of cultural intelligence and discuss how they can become more culturally aware and sensitive in order to interact more effectively with people from diverse backgrounds.

Goals:

- Explain the importance of cross-cultural awareness and sensitivity in today's environment.
- Heighten participants' awareness of cultural intelligence.
- Identify ways to increase cultural intelligence.

Time Required: 20 minutes

Materials and Preparation:

- Prepare five flip chart pages by writing each of the following stages on a separate page and posting them on the walls around the room with plenty of space in between:
  - *Stage 1:* Reaction to external stimuli
  - *Stage 2:* Recognition of other cultural norms and motivation to learn more about them
  - *Stage 3:* Accommodation of other cultural norms and rules in one's own mind
  - *Stage 4:* Assimilation of diverse cultural norms into alternative behaviors
  - *Stage 5:* Proactivity in cultural behavior based on recognition of changing cues that others do not perceive
- *Cultural Intelligence Development Stages* (one per participant)

Process:

1. Introduce the concept of cultural intelligence by explaining that successful leaders have an appreciation for and sensitivity to people from other cultures.
2. Explain that as defined by Thomas and Inkson, authors of *Cultural Intelligence: Living and Working Globally* (2009, p. 153), "Cultural intelligence is the capability to interact effectively with people from different cultural backgrounds."
3. Further explain that there are three components of cultural intelligence:
   Knowledge—understanding of culture and cultural differences
   Mindfulness—paying attention to cues
   Skills—choosing appropriate behavior for the situation

(Continued)

4. Give an example from your own experience to illustrate these components.

5. Distribute the *Cultural Intelligence Development Stages* and ask participants to read carefully the descriptions of the stages of cultural intelligence development. Ask them to put a check mark next to the stage that applies to them. Give them 3 minutes.

6. At the end of the 3 minutes, call time and ask them to get up and position themselves by the flip chart page displayed on the wall that indicates the stage they selected.

7. After people have positioned themselves, ask several volunteers to explain the reason they chose a particular stage.

Discussion:

1. What did you discover about your level of cultural intelligence?

2. What is the reason cultural awareness and sensitivity are important in today's work environment?

3. What can you do to become more culturally aware and sensitive to those whose cultural backgrounds are different from yours?

4. How can cultural awareness and sensitivity help you become more effective as a leader?

Variation:

• If time or space is limited, you may choose to have the participants respond individually at their seats rather than asking them to physically position themselves around the room.

CULTURAL INTELLIGENCE DEVELOPMENT STAGES

Cultural intelligence is developed over time through experience. The following identifies the five stages of cultural intelligence.

STAGE 1: REACTION TO EXTERNAL STIMULI

- You are oblivious to the fact that there are differences among cultures.
- You have had little exposure to or interest in other cultures.

STAGE 2: RECOGNITION OF OTHER CULTURAL NORMS AND MOTIVATION TO LEARN MORE ABOUT THEM

- You have a heightened sense of multiculturalism.
- You struggle to sort through the complexity of the cultural environment.
- You search for simple rules of thumb to guide your behavior.

STAGE 3: ACCOMMODATION OF OTHER CULTURAL NORMS AND RULES IN ONE'S OWN MIND

- A deeper understanding of cultural variation begins to develop.
- Cultural norms and rules of various societies begin to seem comprehensible and even reasonable in their context.
- You begin to recognize appropriate behavioral responses to different cultural situations.
- Adaptive behavior takes lots of effort and is awkward for you.

STAGE 4: ASSIMILATION OF DIVERSE CULTURAL NORMS INTO ALTERNATIVE BEHAVIORS

- Adjusting to different situations no longer requires much effort.
- You have developed a repertoire of behaviors from which you can choose depending on the specific cultural situation.
- You feel at home almost anywhere.

(Continued)

STAGE 5: PROACTIVITY IN CULTURAL BEHAVIOR BASED ON RECOGNITION OF CHANGING CUES THAT OTHERS DO NOT PERCEIVE

- You have the ability to sense changes in cultural context, sometimes even before members of the other cultures do, such as shifts in body language and other nonverbal communication.
- You are attuned to nuances of intercultural interactions, and are able to automatically adjust your behavior.

Source: Adapted from David C. Thomas and Kerr Inkson. (2009). *Cultural Intelligence: Living and Working Globally* (2nd edition). San Francisco: Berrett-Koehler.

DOING IT DIFFERENTLY

Competency: Adaptability/Flexibility/Agility

Description: This activity gives participants an opportunity to explore the concept of adaptability and how it relates to leadership.

Goals:

• Self-assess participants' perceived adaptability.

• Experience how it feels to do something differently.

Time Required: 15 minutes

Materials and Preparation:

• Sets of four three-by-five cards, numbered 1, 2, 3, and 4 (one set per participant)

• Flip chart pages or other visuals, each displaying one of the following written down:

  • I am able to shift gears with minimal stress or difficulty.

  • I see barriers and obstacles as merely temporary setbacks.

  • I try to transform misfortunes into opportunities.

  • I am able to tolerate ambiguity and uncertainty.

  • I adjust my style and approach to work more effectively with others.

• Pens

• Paper

• Markers

• Tent cards

Process:

1. Introduce the activity by explaining that adaptability and flexibility are important leadership characteristics in today's high-pressure, rapidly changing, stressful, and demanding environment.

2. Ask participants to work in pairs and write down examples of situations in which they had to adapt or adjust to different circumstances. Give them 5 minutes.

3. After 5 minutes, solicit examples from the group.

4. Mention that people's ability to adapt can be linked to their personal experiences, their personality traits, and other factors, such as corporate culture. Tell them that you are going to give them the opportunity to reflect on their degree of adaptability.

(Continued)

5. Display the following questions one at a time and ask the participants to hold up the number that best represents their adaptability (1 = Very adaptable; 2 = Moderately adaptable; 3 = Somewhat adaptable; 4 = Not adaptable).
   - I am able to shift gears with minimal stress or difficulty.
   - I see barriers and obstacles as merely temporary setbacks.
   - I try to transform misfortunes into opportunities.
   - I am able to tolerate ambiguity and uncertainty.
   - I adjust my style and approach to work more effectively with others.
6. Ask for volunteers to share their reasons for their responses.
7. Explain that you are now going to engage them in several activities designed to test their adaptability.
8. Choose one or more of the following very brief activities so the participants can experience the ease or difficulty they may have when asked to do something in a different way.
   - Ask each participant to take a sheet of paper and pen and write his or her name using the hand opposite from the one he or she would normally use.
   - Ask participants to fold their arms, unfold them, and then fold them again the opposite way.
   - After a break, move tent cards requiring participants to sit in different places.
   - Ask participants to take off a sweater or jacket and put it back on, making sure they put it on the opposite way they normally would.

Discussion:
1. How did you feel when you did the opposite of what you normally do?
2. What did the activity require you to do that you don't normally have to do?
3. What did you learn about adaptability?
4. What are some things you can do to become more adaptable?
5. How will your ability to be more adaptable help you as a leader?

Variation:
- Rather than ask the participants what they can do to become more adaptable, you might make some of the following suggestions:
  - Take a different route to work.
  - Read articles and books written by people whose viewpoints are different from yours.
  - Try a food you have never eaten before.
  - Do something that is completely uncharacteristic of your temperament or personality.

DO THE RIGHT THING

Competency: Ethics

Description: This activity presents realistic ethical dilemmas that require the participants to respond to the scenarios by drawing on their own values as well as their organization's values and code of ethics.

Goals:

• Distinguish between ethical and unethical behavior.

• Identify the relationship between values and ethics.

Time Required: 60–90 minutes

Materials and Preparation:

• *Do the Right Thing Worksheet* (one per participant)

Process:

1. Introduce the activity by presenting the following background information, paraphrasing or quoting directly: "Ethics are the standards of conduct that guide our behavior. Ethics can be defined both as a set of high moral principles and as behaviors based on one's personal value system. Values define who we are; ethics are what we do. The commitment to conduct business activity lawfully and legally is fundamental to the organization's existence and its success."

2. Ask participants to work in pairs to make a list of the major ethical policy categories or topics and be prepared to explain what each means. Give them 10 minutes.

3. At the end of the 10 minutes, solicit responses. Typical ethics policies address the following areas:

   • Relationships with customers, suppliers, and consultants

   • Gifts or entertainment

   • Conflicts of interest

   • Proprietary information

   • Confidentiality

   • Use of company resources

   • Product integrity

   • Political activity

   • Recording and use of funds

   • Insider trading

(Continued)

4. Next explain that it is important for leaders to understand what is acceptable and unacceptable behavior. Point out that the appropriate response to an ethical dilemma is not always clear-cut. Further explain that they will have an opportunity to gain more insight into the difference between ethical and unethical behavior through a group activity.

5. Distribute copies of the *Do the Right Thing Worksheet* and give them 15 minutes to respond individually to the scenarios.

6. At the end of the 15 minutes, divide the group into subgroups of four or five people and ask them to discuss their responses. Give them 30 minutes.

7. At the end of the designated time period, reconvene the entire group and review the scenarios.

Discussion:

1. What was your reaction to the scenarios?
2. What did you think about or take into consideration as you were discussing the scenarios?
3. How did your responses reflect your personal values?
4. How did your responses reflect your organization's values and ethics policies?
5. What insights did you gain from the activity?
6. How will this information help you in your role as a leader?

Variations:

- For groups from the same organization, distribute copies of the organization's values and ethics policy and ask participants to refer to those documents when responding to the scenarios.
- Solicit from the group examples of other ethical dilemmas they may have encountered.
- If time is limited, assign each subgroup one or two different scenarios rather than all ten.

Do the Right Thing Worksheet

For each of the following scenarios, indicate what action you would take and why.

1. Jane, one of your most tenured and loyal employees, has been taking office supplies home on a regular basis. She is recently divorced and has four small children. Although your company has a strict policy against employees taking supplies for their own personal use, you feel sorry for Jane because you know she is having financial problems. What would you do?

2. You have been invited by a vendor to attend a two-day conference at a five-star resort, all expenses paid. This is a great opportunity to network with your counterparts from other organizations in your industry. What would you do?

3. You have an opportunity to make some additional money by working nights and on the weekends for another company doing the same type of work you do at your full-time job. What would you do?

4. Over the years you have developed a close relationship with one of your vendors. Your son has recently graduated from college and has had no luck finding a job. You casually mention this to the vendor, who says she would be happy to give your son a job. What would you do?

5. You have been asked to submit a proposal for a large contract with a high-profile client. You have recently learned that you are competing with two other companies. Over the course of the preliminary meetings, you and the customer seem to have established a friendly and comfortable relationship. The customer has indicated subtly that he would like to give the business to your firm and has offered to share copies of your competitors' proposals. What would you do?

6. You recently attended a meeting during which the company's new direction was discussed. This new business plan and implementation will result in some major layoffs. Your closest friend works in a department that will be hit the hardest. Your friend senses something is going on and has asked you to share what you know. What would you do?

7. A "headhunter" has contacted you about a very attractive position at another company. In fact, from the description, it sounds as though this could be your dream job. After the preliminary screening, you are one of several candidates the company is considering. The company is anxious to fill this position right away and has requested that you come in the next day for an interview. Your dilemma is that you are expected

(Continued)

to leave tomorrow on a month-long, overseas assignment that cannot be postponed. What would you do?

8. Your company is in cost-cutting mode, and you have been told to cut corners wherever possible. The company has recently licensed a software program that is critical to the efficiency of several departments, including yours. Although your department needs this software, you have been told that there is no money in the budget, and to go ahead and download the software from one of your colleagues. What would you do?

9. You are competing with another company for a prime piece of business. The client tells you who the competitor is and asks you if you know anything about this person. You have heard some very negative things about this particular individual and the company she represents. What would you do?

10. In this very competitive market, you are under a lot of pressure to "do whatever it takes" to increase revenue. One of your most important customers is demanding the delivery of the product within a time frame that cannot be met if quality is to be maintained. Even though you have explained this to the client, he will not budge on the deadline and has threatened to give the business to your competitor if you can't deliver the product on time. What would you do?

FIRED UP!

Competency: Enthusiasm and Passion

Description: This is an individual writing activity that will help participants identify the importance of enthusiasm and passion as leadership characteristics.

Goals:

- Discover the source of participants' personal passion.
- Examine how a leader's passion and enthusiasm can have an impact on others.

Time Required: 30–40 minutes

Materials and Preparation:

- *Fired Up! Individual Worksheet* (one per participant)

Process:

1. Introduce the activity by telling people that passion and enthusiasm are contagious. People who are passionate about what they do and believe in can have a tremendous influence on others. When we are excited or enthusiastic about a cause, task, or project, that enthusiasm spreads to others. Point out that you can't ignite a fire in others unless there is first one burning inside you. Explain that this individual activity is designed to help them identify their passion.
2. Distribute the *Fired Up! Individual Worksheet* and ask people to respond to the questions individually. Give them 10 minutes.
3. At the end of the 10 minutes, ask them to form subgroups of four or five and share their responses with each other. Give them 10 minutes.
4. At the end of the time period, reconvene the entire group and ask for volunteers from each subgroup to share what they learned about passion and enthusiasm through their subgroup discussion.

Discussion:

1. How do passion and enthusiasm relate to leadership?
2. Give examples of leaders who spread their contagious enthusiasm to others. What was the result?
3. How does a person demonstrate passion and enthusiasm?
4. What can you do to ignite your passion or enthusiasm?

(Continued)

5. What can you do to ignite passion in others?

6. What can you do to demonstrate enthusiasm for those things you aren't excited about doing, such as completing unpleasant tasks or implementing decisions that you don't support or agree with?

Variation:

• Ask participants each to develop a personal action plan for igniting passion in others. Form pairs of "accountability partners" and have the pairs agree to follow up with each other after three or four weeks to share how they implemented their plans.

• You can use this activity in an individual coaching session.

FIRED UP! INDIVIDUAL WORKSHEET

Please respond to the following questions. Be as specific as possible.

1. What gets you excited?

2. What energizes you?

3. What makes you want to get up in the morning?

4. What do you sing about in the shower or in the car?

5. What do you dream about?

6. What would you like to do even if you didn't get paid to do it?

HEROES AND HEROINES

Competencies: Influencing, Role Modeling

Description: This activity gives participants an opportunity to think about people who have (or have had) a significant impact on them and how these people have contributed to their success as leaders.

Goals:

- Identify the roles other people play in developing participants' leadership qualities and characteristics.
- Identify how a leader can fulfill these influencing roles for others.

Time Required: 45 minutes

Materials and Preparation:

- *Heroes and Heroines* (one per participant)

Process:

1. Introduce the activity by mentioning that we are all products of our environment, which includes people who have had a significant impact on our lives. These people can be teachers, coaches, friends, parents, neighbors, scout leaders, bosses, colleagues, and so on. People at different times in our lives assume different roles, and their combined influence has resulted in who we are today as people and as leaders.

2. Distribute *Heroes and Heroines*. Ask people to work independently and complete the *Heroes and Heroines* worksheet. As they write the names of the people who fit those roles, ask them to also write down examples of how the people fulfill those roles. Give them 15 minutes.

3. At the end of the 15 minutes, form subgroups of four or five and ask the participants to share with each other one person from their list and the impact that person has had on their life. Give them 15 minutes.

4. At the end of the 15-minute discussion period, reconvene the entire group and solicit examples for each of the categories.

Discussion:

1. What was your reaction to the activity?

2. What did you learn about the roles others play in developing your leadership characteristics and competencies?

3. How can you apply these same qualities and characteristics to your role as a leader?

Variation:

- This can be given as an assignment for the participants to complete prior to the classroom session.

HEROES AND HEROINES LIST

Think about the people who have (or have had) a significant impact on your professional or personal life. For each of the following roles, identify the person or people who fulfill that role for you. Also, give specific examples of what they do (or did) to fill those roles.

1. **Coaches** help you improve your performance or skill level. They help you increase your proficiency or expertise in a particular area.
2. **Cheerleaders** provide emotional support. They are there to "cheer you on" and give you encouragement.
3. **Role models** are people you admire, look up to, and emulate. They can be people you don't even know.
4. **Thought provokers** challenge your thoughts, beliefs, and positions. They push you to think "outside the box," to try new ways of doing things.
5. **Critics** give you honest, constructive feedback. They tell you what other people may be afraid to tell you.
6. **Igniters** inspire you. They are people you want to emulate because of their own accomplishments and abilities.
7. **Promoters** spread the word about you. They tell others about your accomplishments and abilities.
8. **Counselors** give advice about problems. They are people with whom you can address personal issues that may be hampering your effectiveness.
9. **Champions** help you get ahead. They actively support you and defend you when others criticize you.
10. **Advisers** offer suggestions. They share insights and make recommendations, primarily in regard to business-related issues.

LIVING YOUR VALUES

Competency: Congruence

Description: The purpose of this activity is to give participants insight into the values that drive their behavior, and to examine how a person's behavior reflects his or her values.

Goals:

- Identify behavior that supports or contradicts one's values.
- Identify congruence between actions and values.

Time Required: 60 minutes

Materials and Preparation:

- *Living Your Values Worksheet* (one per participant)
- *Living Your Values Discussion Sheet* (one per participant)

Process:

1. Introduce the activity by discussing the concept of congruence as it relates to values and behavior. Solicit from the group examples in which a person's actions or behavior did not support her or her proclaimed values.
2. Distribute the *Living Your Values Worksheet* and ask participants to complete it individually, writing down specific examples of your behavior that support or contradict each value. Give them 20 minutes.
3. At the end of the 20 minutes, divide the group into subgroups of four or five. Distribute the *Living Your Values Discussion Sheet*. Explain that you will give them 15 minutes to discuss the questions, and tell them that they do not have to share any information unless they want to.
4. At the end of the 15 minutes, reconvene the entire group and solicit feedback about the questions on the *Living Your Values Discussion Sheet*.

Discussion:

1. What was your reaction to the activity?
2. What did you learn about yourself?
3. What are you going to do differently to make sure your behavior is "in sync" with your values?

(Continued)

Variations:

- You may choose to delete items from or add to the list of values on the *Living Your Values Worksheet*.
- To add another dimension to the activity, you may ask participants to rank the values, with number 1 being the most important.

LIVING YOUR VALUES WORKSHEET

Value	My Behavior Supporting That Value	My Behavior Contradicting That Value
Knowledge and wisdom To learn new things and ideas		
Morality and ethics To maintain a sense of right and wrong and personal integrity		
Freedom and independence To be able to make one's own decisions and use one's own judgment		
Money and security To have enough income and resources to provide for wants and needs		
Mental and physical health To be free of stress, anxiety, and physical illness; to be fit and energetic		
Religious beliefs and spirituality To believe in a supreme being or spiritual force		
Friendships and relationships To have a sense of belonging to a person or group; to care for others		

(Continued)

Pleasure and enjoyment To participate in things one likes to do; to have fun and enjoy life		
Achievement and accomplishment To have a feeling of self-satisfaction as a result of completing a task, overcoming an obstacle, or meeting a challenge		
Loyalty and trust To experience a feeling of dedication and commitment to friends, family, country, organization, and so on		
Respect and civility To value and appreciate others; to be considerate and courteous		
Justice and equity To believe in a system that rewards positive behavior and punishes negative behavior; to have a sense of fairness		

LIVING YOUR VALUES DISCUSSION SHEET

1. What are some examples of your behavior that were not congruent with your values?

2. What is the personal impact when one's behavior is not congruent with his or her stated values?

3. What is the impact on others when a leader's behavior is not congruent with his or her stated values?

4. What might cause a person to behave in a way that violates his or her values?

5. How do your values influence your decisions, personally and professionally?

MIRROR, MIRROR

Competency: Self-Awareness

Description: This is an individual activity in which participants increase their self-awareness by completing a self-assessment and then comparing it to the feedback from others.

Goals:

- Identify participants' strengths and shortcomings through self-assessment and feedback from others.
- Develop personal action plans to increase participants' effectiveness in their relationships with others.

Time Required: Varies

Materials and Preparation:

- *Mirror, Mirror Self-Assessment* (one per participant)
- *Mirror, Mirror Feedback* (one per participant)

Process:

1. Introduce the activity by telling participants that effective leaders are keenly aware of their strengths as well as their shortcomings. They are not afraid to solicit and listen to feedback from those whom they trust to be honest in delivering it.
2. Tell them that they will have an opportunity to identify their perceived strengths and their shortcomings through a self-assessment and feedback process.
3. Distribute the *Mirror, Mirror Self-Assessment* and ask them to spend 20 minutes responding to the questions.
4. At the end of the 20 minutes, ask for volunteers to share their reaction to completing the assessment.
5. Next, distribute *Mirror, Mirror Feedback* and ask them to identify one or more people outside of the session they would trust to give them honest feedback. Instruct participants to make copies and distribute the forms to those from whom they are seeking feedback, and have them collect the feedback forms prior to the next session.
6. During the next session, conduct a general discussion about the value of the activity.

Discussion:

1. What did you learn about yourself?
2. How was the feedback you received similar to or different from your self-assessment?

3. What are some areas you have identified as opportunities for improvement?

4. How can you use this information to be more effective as a leader?

Variations:

• Rather than asking another person or other people to complete the feedback version, participants could complete the feedback form by speculating on how others would respond.

• This could be given as an assignment to be completed prior to the classroom session.

• You can use this activity as an assignment in a one-on-one coaching situation.

MIRROR, MIRROR SELF-ASSESSMENT

Effective leaders are keenly self-aware. They are in touch with both their strengths and their shortcomings, and they are not afraid to solicit and listen to feedback from those whom they trust in delivering it. In an effort to increase your self-awareness, please respond to the following questions.

Then make copies of the *Mirror, Mirror Feedback* form, and ask one or more people to complete it and return it to you so that you can compare your self-perception with the perception of others and develop a personal action plan to increase your personal effectiveness.

1. What words would you use to describe yourself?

2. How would you describe your interpersonal communication skills?

3. What are your greatest strengths in working with and interacting with others?

4. What are your greatest shortcomings when interacting with others?

5. What do you think you could do to be more effective in building relationships?

Mirror, Mirror Feedback

Subject's Name: Your Name:

The person named above is engaged in an activity to identify his or her perceived strengths and shortcomings through a self-assessment and feedback process. This person is asking you to provide feedback to him or her by completing the following questionnaire. Please be honest and candid in your responses.

1. What words would you use to describe this person?

2. How would you describe his or her interpersonal communication skills?

3. What are his or her greatest strengths in working and interacting with others?

4. What are his or her greatest shortcomings when interacting with others?

5. What would you like to see him or her do (or do differently) when interacting with others?

6. How could he or she be more effective in building relationships?

MODELING THE WAY

Competencies: Congruence, Role Modeling

Description: This brief activity is an excellent way of introducing the topics of congruence and role modeling.

Goals:

- Recognize the importance of congruent behavior as a leadership characteristic.
- Explore the impact of a leader's incongruent behavior on employees.
- Identify ways in which a leader can demonstrate congruent behavior.

Time Required: 15–20 minutes

Materials and Preparation:

- *Modeling the Way Discussion Sheet* (one per participant)

Process:

1. Begin the activity by telling the participants that very often we can find lessons in leadership from classic literature, such as in myths, fables, Shakespeare's plays, and so on. Ask participants if they can think of any examples of leadership lessons.

2. Tell them that *Aesop's Fables* has many good life lessons that are applicable to today's leaders. One such fable is "The Crab and Its Mother." Ask them to listen carefully as you read the fable and then be ready to discuss its message or application.

   "A Crab said to her son, 'Why do you walk so one-sided, my child? It is far more becoming to go straight forward.' The young Crab replied: 'Quite true, dear Mother; and if you will show me the straight way, I will promise to walk in it.' The Mother tried in vain, and submitted without remonstrance [protest] to the reproof of her child" (*Aesop's Fables*, 1968, p. 86).

3. After you have read the fable, distribute the *Modeling the Way Discussion Sheet* to the participants. Divide the group into subgroups of four or five and ask them to discuss the questions on the handout. Give them 5 to 7 minutes.

4. At the end of the time period, reconvene the group and conduct a discussion of the lesson about leadership gleaned from the fable, using the discussion sheet as a guideline. Make sure that the discussion focuses on the concept of "actions speak louder than words" and on how important it is to model the behavior you expect from others.

Discussion:

1. What did you learn from the fable?
2. How do you see this behavior of role modeling demonstrated in the workplace?
3. What can you do to demonstrate and model the behavior you expect from others?

Variation:

• This can be given as an individual assignment.

MODELING THE WAY DISCUSSION SHEET

1. What was the lesson or main message of the fable?

2. How does the fable's lesson relate to a leader and his or her followers?

3. What are some examples you have witnessed as a follower in which the behavior of the leader was much like that of the young crab's mother?

4. What was the impact of the behavior on you and other followers?

Permission or Forgiveness?

Competency: Risk Taking

Description: This point-counterpoint activity engages participants in a discussion of risk taking and its relationship to leadership.

Goal:

• Examine participants' attitudes toward risk taking.

Time Required: 10 minutes

Materials and Preparation:

• Slide or flip chart page on which the following appears: "It is better to ask for forgiveness than permission."

Process:

1. Introduce the activity by telling participants that they will have an opportunity to examine attitudes toward risk taking through a point-counterpoint activity.
2. Display the following statement on a flip chart page or slide: "It is better to ask for forgiveness than permission."
3. Divide the group into two subgroups.
4. Ask one subgroup to discuss and come up with points in support of the statement.
5. Ask the other subgroup to prepare arguments against the statement.
6. Give the subgroups 3 minutes to prepare their arguments or key points.
7. At the end of the 3 minutes, call time. Begin the discussion by asking a person from the subgroup in support of the statement to offer one key point. Then ask that person to call on someone in the other subgroup to offer a counterpoint.
8. Continue this back-and-forth, "call-on-the-next-speaker" format for 3 minutes.
9. At the end of the 3 minutes, lead a discussion about what participants learned about their (and others') attitudes toward risk taking.

Discussion:

1. What was your reaction to the activity?
2. How did you feel if you had to take a position with which you did not agree?
3. What was your reaction when you heard some of the arguments from the other side?

(Continued)

4. How does this experience relate to risk taking?
5. What insights did you gain about people's attitudes toward risk taking?
6. What are some examples of times when you have demonstrated "asking for forgiveness" rather than "asking for permission"? What was the outcome?

Variation:

• Rather than conducting a point-counterpoint discussion, you could put people in subgroups to discuss the meaning of the statement and give specific examples from their own experience.

RISK ATTITUDES INVENTORY

Competency: Risk Taking

Description: This self-assessment gives participants an opportunity to examine their own attitudes toward risk taking and to explore the relationship between risk taking and leadership effectiveness.

Goals:

- Assess participants' risk-taking traits.
- Identify participants' assumptions about the consequences of risk taking.

Time Required: 45 minutes

Materials and Preparation:

- *Risk Attitudes Inventory* (one per participant)
- *Risk Attitudes Inventory Interpretation* (one per participant)

Process:

1. Explain that successful leaders are those who take risks.
2. Explain to participants that the first step toward increasing their willingness and ability to take risks is a self-assessment. You are going to give them an opportunity to examine their own attitudes toward risk taking.
3. Distribute the *Risk Attitudes Inventory.* Explain that this survey is a general tool to stimulate reflection and thought about one's risk-taking style and beliefs, and that it is not a rigid, diagnostic instrument. Give them 10 minutes to complete the assessment and score it.
4. Distribute the *Risk Attitudes Inventory Interpretation* and ask the participants to spend a few minutes reviewing the interpretation of each item.
5. Reconvene the group and explain that the higher their score, the more their risk-taking attitudes resemble those of risk takers studied by social scientists. A score of 11 or higher indicates strong to very strong pro-risk attitudes; 6 to 10, medium-strength pro-risk attitudes; and 5 or lower, low-strength pro-risk attitudes.

Discussion:

1. What was your reaction to completing this self-assessment?
2. What did you learn about your willingness and ability to take risks?

(Continued)

3. How is risk regarded in your organization?

4. What is your reaction to (or perception of) people who take risks?

5. What is your perception of the relationship between risk taking and leadership effectiveness?

Variation:

- This assessment can be given as an assignment for the participants to complete prior to the classroom session.

- You can use this self-assessment in an individual coaching session.

RISK ATTITUDES INVENTORY QUESTIONNAIRE

By Gene Calvert

Read each trait description. Assess yourself on the basis of the degree to which the trait description applies to you (most of the time) in your management work and circle the appropriate answer. Be aware that looking for hidden meanings will not improve the values of your self-rating. Your first reaction is probably your best.

1. Taking management risks makes good sense only in the absence of acceptable alternatives. — Agree   Disagree
2. I generally prefer stimulation over security. — Agree   Disagree
3. I have confidence in my ability to recover from my mistakes, no matter how big. — Agree   Disagree
4. I would promote someone with unlimited potential but limited experience to a key position over someone with limited potential but more experience. — Agree   Disagree
5. Anything worth doing is worth doing less than perfectly. — Agree   Disagree
6. I believe that opportunity generally knocks only once. — Agree   Disagree
7. It is better to ask for permission than to beg for forgiveness. — Agree   Disagree
8. Success in management is as much a matter of luck as ability. — Agree   Disagree
9. I would choose a three-thousand-dollar annual raise over a ten-thousand-dollar bonus, when I had about a one-in-three chance of winning the bonus. — Agree   Disagree
10. I can handle big losses and disappointments with little difficulty. — Agree   Disagree
11. If forced to choose between them, I would take safety over achievement. — Agree   Disagree
12. Failure is the long road to management success. — Agree   Disagree
13. I tolerate ambiguity and unpredictability well. — Agree   Disagree
14. I would rather feel intense disappointment than intense regret. — Agree   Disagree
15. When facing a decision with uncertain consequences, my potential losses are my greatest concern. — Agree   Disagree

(Continued)

Scoring:

Give yourself one point for each of the following statements with which you agree:
2, 3, 4, 5, 10, 13, 14
Give yourself one point for each of the following questions with which you disagree:
1, 6, 7, 8, 9, 11, 12, 15
Calculate your total.

Source: Highwire Management by Gene Calvert. Copyright 1993 by Jossey-Bass Publishers (pages 43–44).
Reprinted with permission.

Risk Attitudes Inventory Interpretation

Your score will tell you more about your risk-taking attitudes when you compare your responses with those of a risk taker. Someone giving a pro-risk response on all inventory items would agree with the following beliefs and assumptions about risk taking, which correspond to the items in the inventory.

1. Risk by choice, not just by necessity; chosen risks usually benefit you much more than forced ones.

2. Security is a myth; professional stimulation (challenge, growth or excitement) is worth the cost.

3. A way out of almost any risk-taking problem can probably be found or created, including a way to survive "the worst," if it actually happens. I have skills to deal with risk.

4. Conventional personnel management practices like promoting someone on the basis of past experience, generally produces average results, if more certain performance; unconventional management practices like promoting someone on the basis of his or her potential produce unconventional results such as outstanding, if sometimes less certain, performance.

5. Risk taking is typically a messy, fast-moving, make-it-up-as-you-go, very imperfect process, no matter how well you plan or implement it; waiting until you can risk near-perfectly means seldom risking or missing the best window of opportunity for risking.

6. No matter how many times your risks fail, there will always be another opportunity to risk again and perhaps succeed the next time. The ratio of wins to losses matters little in the end. Risk takers know that what counts most is the net total value of wins compared to losses in an acceptable period of time, such as a budget cycle or an average time span at a management position or level.

7. While getting permission is always a smart move, some management risks have to be launched without prior approval; if it succeeds, no apologies are needed; if the risk fails, and it was legitimate and responsibly undertaken, you will probably be forgiven anyway.

8. Luck always helps, but you create your own luck by taking risks and betting on yourself. Your own ability contributes to making things happen the way you want them to

(Continued)

happen. "You have to play to win"; for managers, that means taking risks and not depending on random circumstances, events, or other people.

9. The bigger the risk, the bigger the reward, so go for the riskier choice if it offers a greater payoff; believe in your own ability to produce results, especially when you have pivotal control of the outcome, as with your job performance.

10. Failure and loss should be viewed as learning experiences that will pay off in the long term. What you learn from your risk-taking mistakes is what makes risks worth taking. Learning anything new is a matter of doing things wrong until you get them right.

11. For a manager or an organization, achieving anything worthwhile requires venturing into unsafe territory. Being satisfied with average achievements, a standard of mediocrity, allows you to stick with the safe, sure, and secure; being dissatisfied with anything less than outstanding, a standard of excellence, forces you to relinquish the safe, sure, and secure.

12. Succeeding as a manager means having a modest share of failures, if only because producing outstanding results requires taking risks, many of which will fail. The trick is not to fail too catastrophically.

13. Ambiguity and unpredictability permeate and complicate risk taking; those able to cope with these constraints will do well at risk taking, or at least better than those who can't.

14. You always feel good about yourself when you risk sensibly and boldly, even if you fail, for you sustain and expand your self-esteem and earn the respect of others. Risking and then failing means never having to blame yourself for lacking the courage to try. Better to feel the disappointments of risking than the regrets of not risking.

15. When risking, keep one eye on the potential losses and one on the potential gains, instead of focusing obsessively on what you can lose. Risk to secure gains, as well as to prevent losses.

Source: Highwire Management by Gene Calvert. Copyright 1993 by Jossey-Bass Publishers (pages 44–46). Reprinted with permission.

THE BALANCING ACT

Competency: Balancing Personal and Professional

Description: This activity is effective in helping participants clarify what is important to them and identify possible reasons for stress in their lives. It further provides them with the opportunity to set specific goals and develop strategies to improve their quality of life.

Goals:

• Analyze participants' current state of work-life balance.

• Identify specific ways to improve participants' work-life balance.

Time Required: 45–60 minutes

Materials and Preparation:

• *Life Wheel* (one per participant)

• *Setting Goals* (one per participant)

Process:

1. Introduce the activity by explaining that our lives can be broken down into seven categories: career and professional; spiritual; mental and intellectual; social and recreational; physical; family; and financial.

2. Distribute the *Life Wheel* and briefly provide the following explanations of each category:

   Career and professional refers not only to your current job but also to what you want to do professionally in the long term.

   Spiritual refers to formal religious activities or to anything of a spiritual nature, such as meditation.

   Mental and intellectual refers to activities that engage your mind, such as nonrecreational reading or specific, intellectually stimulating endeavors like attending classes to complete a degree or broaden your knowledge in a particular area.

   Social and recreational refers to activities you might engage in with others, such as going out to dinner, movies, the theater, or sports events with friends; engaging in some recreational or sports activity; taking a vacation; or just spending time by yourself pursuing a hobby, such as reading, flower arranging, model building, and so on.

   Physical refers to all aspects of your physical being and includes exercise, sleep, and nutrition.

(Continued)

Family refers to the amount of time you spend with members of your family, such as your spouse, significant other, children, parents, and other family members.

Financial refers to your current financial requirements and behaviors (salary, budgeting, savings, investing, housing) as well as your future financial needs and concerns (money for children's education, retirement, net worth, and so on).

3. Refer the participants to the "balanced" life wheel on the handout, pointing out that each of the seven sections is the same size. Mention, however, that the reality is that each person's wheel will be different depending on his or her situation.

4. Ask each participant to draw his or her wheel as it is today, keeping in mind the seven sections. In other words, participants must determine how much time, energy, and effort are devoted to each life category and then draw the appropriate-size wedge. Emphasize that this estimate is purely subjective. Also mention that some categories may not even appear on the wheel, and some may be depicted as mere slivers.

5. After each person has completed his or her "current" life wheel, direct each participant to create his or her "ideal" wheel—that is, to draw the life wheel as the person would like it to be.

6. After all participants have completed their wheels, have them form pairs. Ask them to spend 3 or 4 minutes each sharing with their partner what they learned about themselves by comparing their "current" and "ideal" wheels.

7. At the end of 8 minutes, reconvene the entire group and ask them to indicate by a show of hands how many of them had a difference between the two wheels. Then ask them what happens when the two wheels are "out of sync." The responses should indicate that stress and frustration result.

8. Explain that although very few people probably ever reach their "ideal" wheel state, each person can take specific steps to create a "current" wheel that is closer to his or her "ideal" wheel. The key is in setting specific goals and developing specific action steps or strategies to meet those goals.

9. Distribute *Setting Goals* and explain that each participant is going to have an opportunity to begin to take specific action to improve his or her work-life situation.

10. Divide the group into subgroups of two or three, and assign each subgroup one or more of the life categories depending on the number of subgroups you have.

11. Explain that for each of the assigned categories, subgroup members are to write a specific goal or objective, along with the strategies or action steps they would take to reach

that goal or objective. They can use a real example from one of the subgroup members, or they can make up an example. To clarify, offer an example, such as the following:

Category: Physical

Goal: Get in better physical shape.

Objective: Lose thirty pounds in four months.

Strategies: Beginning next week, join a gym and follow a 30- to 45-minute workout at least three times a week.

Objective: Eat three balanced meals each day.

Strategies: Beginning this Saturday, write out a meal plan for the entire following week; make a grocery list; go to the grocery store to purchase the ingredients for the week's meals. Continue to do this every week.

12. After the subgroups have completed the assignment, reconvene the entire group and ask a spokesperson from each group to share his or her subgroup's goals, objectives, and strategies for the assigned categories. As you listen to each subgroup report out, be sure to press for specifics, such as time frames.

Discussion:

1. What did you experience as you were drawing your "current" and "ideal" wheels?
2. What did you experience as you were working in your subgroup to develop goals, objectives, and strategies for your assigned categories?
3. What did you learn about yourself from this activity?
4. What are you going to do differently?
5. How can this activity help you gain control over your life and reduce stress?

Variation:

• This activity can be completed by an individual in a nonclassroom setting.

LIFE WHEEL

"Balanced" Life Wheel:

"Current" Life Wheel: Please draw your life wheel as it is today.

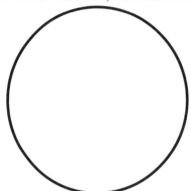

"Ideal" Life Wheel: Please draw your life wheel as you would like it to be.

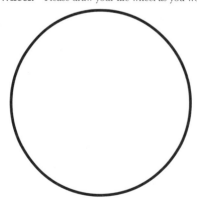

SETTING GOALS

Your life comprises many different areas. To be a happy and fulfilled person, you need to carefully examine and set goals for each area of your life. For each of the following life categories, identify two or three goals or objectives. Then write specific strategies to help you reach those goals. Remember that a goal or objective needs to be **S**pecific, **M**easurable, **A**ttainable/Achievable, **R**ealistic, and **T**ime-bound.

Category	Goals/Objectives	Strategies
Career/professional		
Spiritual		
Mental/intellectual		
Social/recreational		
Physical		
Family		
Financial		

Strategies for achieving these goals and objectives should be included in your daily or long-term "to do" list.

Source: "The Balancing Act: An Activity for Creating Work-Life Balance" by Karen Lawson in *2002 Training and Performance Sourcebook* (pages 21–27). Mel Silberman, Editor. 2002. Reproduced with permission of McGraw-Hill.

VALUES COLLAGE

Competency: Clarifying Values

Description: This activity helps participants gain insights into the values that drive their behavior and decisions.

Goals:

- Clarify participants' personal values.
- Examine how participants' values relate to their roles as leaders.

Time Required: 45–60 minutes

Materials and Preparation:

- Variety of magazines with lots of pictures
- Scissors (one per participant)
- Glue (one per participant)
- Standard poster board pieces, cut in half (one per participant)
- Markers

Process:

1. Introduce the activity by explaining that, in many cases, the organization's values reflect those of its leaders. Effective leaders are clear about their personal values as well as those of the organization. Our values guide our decisions and are the very core of who we are. Although our values help define who we are and influence what we do, many of us have never had the opportunity to think about and examine closely what we value and why. Explain that this activity is designed to give participants insights into the values that drive their behavior.

2. Distribute scissors, glue, markers, magazines, and pieces of poster board to the participants. Tell them that they are to use these resources to create a collage that represents their personal values. The collage may have both words and pictures. Tell them they have 25 minutes to complete their project and be ready to display it for the entire group.

3. At the end of the 25 minutes, call time and ask each person to display his or her collage and briefly explain what it represents.

Discussion:

1. What was your reaction to creating the collage?
2. What did you discover about yourself?

3. How do these values reflect your behavior as a leader?

4. How do your personal values match the values of your organization?

5. What is the benefit of this activity?

6. How can you use these insights into your (and others') values in your role as a leader?

Variations:

• In a multisession program, this can be a "take-home" assignment between sessions.

• Rather than giving this as an individual assignment, depending on the makeup of your group you could create subgroups by department, organization, position, generation, and so on and ask each one to create a group collage that represents the values of the group.

• If time is limited, you may choose to have only a few volunteers show their collages, or you could simply ask all participants to display the collages around the room or at their tables and allow a few minutes for the participants to walk around and view each other's work.

WHAT IS IT LIKE?

Competencies: Empathy, Motivating, Relationship Building

Description: This rotating trio role-play activity is designed to enhance the participants' understanding of and sensitivity to other people and their circumstances.

Goals:

- Increase participants' awareness of and sensitivity to others.
- Identify situations in which a leader should demonstrate his or her ability to empathize.

Time Required: 60 minutes

Materials and Preparation:

- *Manager's Role Assignment*
  - *Round 1 Manager's Role—"Stressed Out"* (one per trio)
  - *Round 2 Manager's Role—"Not Appreciated"* (one per trio)
  - *Round 3 Manager's Role—"Unfairly Criticized"* (one per trio)
- *Employee's Role Assignment*
  - *Round 1 Employee's Role—"Stressed Out"* (one per trio)
  - *Round 2 Employee's Role—"Not Appreciated"* (one per trio)
  - *Round 3 Employee's Role—"Unfairly Criticized"* (one per trio)
- *Observer's Sheet* (one per participant)

Process:

1. Introduce the activity by asking participants to define empathy and provide examples. Clarify as needed by explaining that empathy is the ability to "put yourself in another person's shoes—that is, to understand where that person 'is coming from' and to communicate that understanding." Explain that they will engage in an activity that will give them the opportunity to explore situations from another person's perspective.

2. Divide the group into trios. Explain that this activity will consist of three 5-minute rounds. In each round, each member of the trio will assume the role of manager, employee, or observer. Ask them to decide which role they want for each round.

3. Distribute the *Observer's Sheet* and review it with the group, pointing out that when they are observing the role-play, they should note specific behavior examples on the part of both the manager and the employee.

4. Distribute the *Round 1 Manager's Role* and the *Round 1 Employee's Role* to each trio. Tell them they have 5 minutes.

5. At the end of the 5 minutes, call time. Repeat the process for Round 2 and Round 3.

6. At the end of Round 3, reconvene the entire group and facilitate a discussion of the activity.

Discussion:

1. What did you experience in the role of the manager? How did you feel?

2. What did you experience in the role of the employee? How did you feel?

3. What did you notice in your role as the observer?

4. How realistic were these scenarios?

5. What situations do you encounter (or have you encountered) that are similar to these scenarios?

6. How have you handled situations like these in the past?

7. How does this activity underscore the importance of empathy as a leadership characteristic?

8. What might you do differently as a result of experiencing this activity?

Variation:

• If time is limited and you have at least three trios, assign each trio a different scenario and conduct only one round.

MANAGER'S ROLE ASSIGNMENT

ROUND 1 MANAGER'S ROLE— "STRESSED OUT"

You have a major, high-profile project with a tight deadline that is behind schedule. You are also experiencing a staff shortage and expect everyone on your team to do whatever is necessary to complete this project, even if it means working longer hours and over the weekend. You have the same expectations for each employee, regardless of his or her personal circumstances. You are to approach your employee and explain the situation and your expectations.

ROUND 2 MANAGER'S ROLE— "NOT APPRECIATED"

Your department has been tapped to work on a special project that is critical to the organization. This project is going to require extra time and effort on the part of all your employees. Because of the importance of this project, you approach the person you can always count on to take on the additional responsibility of managing the project.

ROUND 3 MANAGER'S ROLE— "UNFAIRLY CRITICIZED"

You are under a lot of pressure from your boss to prepare and submit a proposal for a large contract. In order to prepare this proposal, you need some important information from one of your employees, who is a day late in getting the information to you. You approach the employee in his or her work station and make it quite clear you are not happy that you do not have the requested information. You are not interested in hearing any excuses.

Employee's Role Assignment

Round 1 Employee's Role—"Stressed Out"

You are a dedicated and hardworking employee, but you are experiencing a great deal of stress in your personal life. Because you have some other binding commitments and family responsibilities, you can't work overtime.

Round 2 Employee's Role—"Not Appreciated"

You are a dedicated and hardworking employee and consider yourself a real team player, frequently staying late to help your colleagues when they are overburdened. Although you never complain, it seems as though you are expected to do more than your colleagues.

Round 3 Employee's Role—"Unfairly Criticized"

You are a dedicated and hardworking employee, taking pride in your work and making it a point to meet deadlines and fulfill your other job responsibilities. You have been hampered the last two days from getting the information your boss requested due to computer problems.

Observer's Sheet

1. How did the manager approach the employee?

2. What was the employee's reaction?

3. To what degree did the manager modify his or her approach during the discussion based on the employee's reaction?

WHO AM I?

Competency: Self-Awareness

Description: This self-assessment activity gives participants an opportunity to explore the four basic personality types or styles, and to consider how these styles influence behavior in the workplace.

Goals:

- Identify participants' primary personality style or styles.
- Recognize the personality styles of others.
- Identify ways for a leader to adapt his or her behavior to be more effective in his or her role.

Time Required: 60 minutes

Materials and Preparation:

- *Personality Profile Assessment* (one per participant)
- *Personality Profile Interpretation* (one per participant)
- Flip chart pages
- Markers

Process:

1. Introduce the activity by commenting that effective leaders are acutely self-aware.
2. Explain that each participant is going to have an opportunity to identify his or her primary personality profile, including characteristics and behaviors.
3. Distribute the *Personality Profile Assessment* and ask participants to complete the assessment according to the written instructions.
4. After the participants have completed scoring the assessment, distribute the *Personality Profile Interpretation* and ask participants to read the description of their preferred style as determined by the letter they circled the most.
5. Group them according to their styles. In cases in which a participant has two styles that dominate, ask the participant to choose which style is more descriptive of him or her and then join that particular group. (Note: Some participants may not agree with their results. Point out that they created their own data, so if they disagree, they may want to revisit their responses to the items.)

(Continued)

6. Ask subgroup members to develop two lists for their style as it relates to their roles as leaders: (1) strengths and (2) potential weaknesses or shortcomings. Give them 10 minutes to complete their lists and post them on flip chart pages.

7. Reconvene the entire group and invite the participants to review each subgroup's lists.

8. Solicit examples of how these strengths and weaknesses can have an impact on their roles as leaders.

9. Point out that in addition to being aware of their own style, they need to be aware of, understand, and adjust to the styles of others. They will influence others through their ability to adjust their style to those of others. Also, their acceptance of others and their willingness to adapt will influence others to accept and adapt to them as well.

Discussion:

1. What was your reaction to completing the profile?
2. What was your reaction to reading the interpretation?
3. To what degree do you agree or disagree with the results?
4. If you have completed other similar assessments, to what degree are these results similar to or different from those of the others?
5. What insights did you gain about yourself?
6. How can you use these insights to help you become a more effective leader?

Variations:

- Instead of using the *Personality Profile Assessment,* you may choose to use another assessment that identifies four different styles.
- You may also suggest that participants create a 360-degree process by asking others (direct reports, bosses, colleagues, and so on) to complete the assessment of them.

PERSONALITY PROFILE ASSESSMENT

Read each of the following statements and circle the ending that describes you the best.

1. When I am in a learning situation, I like to . . .
   a. Be involved in doing something
   b. Work with people in groups
   c. Read about the information
   d. Watch and listen to what is going on

2. When I am working in a group, I like to . . .
   a. Direct the discussion and activity
   b. Find out what other people think and feel
   c. Remain somewhat detached from the rest of the group
   d. Go along with the majority

3. When faced with a conflict situation, I prefer to . . .
   a. Confront the situation head-on and try to win
   b. Work with the other person to arrive at an amicable resolution
   c. Present my position by using logic and reason
   d. Not make waves

4. In a conversation, I tend to . . .
   a. Come straight to the point
   b. Draw others into the conversation
   c. Listen to what others have to say, then offer an objective opinion
   d. Agree with what others say

5. When making a decision, I tend to . . .
   a. Make a decision quickly and then move on
   b. Consider how the outcome will affect others
   c. Take time to gather facts and data
   d. Consider all possible outcomes and proceed with caution

6. I am seen by others as someone who . . .
   a. Gets results
   b. Is fun to be with
   c. Is logical and rational
   d. Is a calming influence

(Continued)

7. In a work environment, I prefer . . .
    a. To work alone
    b. To work with others
    c. Structure and organization
    d. A peaceful atmosphere

Now count the number of times you circled each letter. The letter with the most circles indicates your preferred style: a = Candid; b = Persuasive; c = Logical; d = Reflective.

PERSONALITY PROFILE INTERPRETATION

As you read the following brief descriptions, determine for yourself the accuracy of the description as it reflects your personality style.

CANDID

Candid individuals are direct and controlling. They like to be in charge and the center of attention. They are action-oriented and may be perceived as pushy and domineering. They enjoy being challenged, and they tend to make decisions quickly, sometimes with little information. Those with the candid style are demanding of themselves and others.

Words associated with the candid style are *dominant, driving*, and *direct*.

To be more effective, the candid person needs to be more sensitive to others, practice active listening, and exercise more caution in making decisions.

PERSUASIVE

Those whose primary style is persuasive love people. They are outgoing, warm, and animated. They are very sociable and may be perceived as overly emotional. They have a short attention span and dislike details. Persuasive individuals are spontaneous, are entertaining, and like to take risks.

Words associated with the persuasive style are *amiable, influencing*, and *expressive*.

To be more effective, the persuasive person needs to improve communication skills and spend more time looking at the facts.

LOGICAL

Logical individuals pride themselves on their use of analysis and reason in all situations. They have a strong need to be right, and they rely on facts and data to support their position. Although they are good problem solvers, they are slow to make decisions. They are sometimes perceived as aloof and critical. They often ask probing questions, and frequently take the opposite point of view in a discussion.

Words associated with the logical style are *steady, systematic*, and *thinking*.

To be more effective, the logical person needs to be more flexible, spend less time gathering data, show more concern for people, and be more expressive of his or her feelings.

(Continued)

REFLECTIVE

Reflective individuals are reliable and cautious. They tend to be perfectionists and seek security. They avoid conflict, and may be perceived by others as weak. Reflective people are good listeners and make great friends. They are loyal, cooperative, and supportive. For this reason, they are good team players.

Words associated with the reflective style are *conscientious, considerate,* and *amiable.*

To be more effective, the reflective person should learn to be more assertive, less sensitive, and more willing to take risks.

CHAPTER FIVE

COMMUNICATING AND INFLUENCING

Communicating and influencing are skills critical to the leader's success. In addition to being able to express themselves well, successful leaders are good listeners and observers. They also know how to pull valuable information from people by asking the right questions. The activities in this chapter are designed to help leaders enhance their communication skills to increase their influence with others.

ACTIVE LISTENING RESPONSES

Competency: Listening

Description: This activity is designed to help participants become more skillful at giving active listening responses.

Goals:

- Increase awareness of the active listening process.
- Develop appropriate active listening responses to people's concerns, ideas, problems, and feelings.

Time Required: 20 minutes

Materials and Preparation:

- *Active Listening Responses* (one per participant)

Process:

1. Introduce the activity by mentioning that active listening is an important but forgotten skill. Share the following information with the participants: studies show that we spend 80 percent of our waking hours communicating, and according to research, at least 45 percent of that time is spent listening. Although listening is a primary activity, most individuals are inefficient listeners. Tests have shown that immediately after listening to a 10-minute oral presentation, the average listener has heard, understood, properly evaluated, and retained approximately half of what was said. And within 48 hours, that drops off another 50 percent to a final 25 percent level of effectiveness. In other words, we comprehend and retain only one-quarter of what was said.

   Furthermore, studies show that most leaders are poor listeners. In a 2006 survey of 1,400 leaders, managers, and executives conducted by the Ken Blanchard companies, 41 percent said that inappropriate use of communication or listening is the number one mistake leaders make. Eighty-one percent indicated that they were not satisfied with their ability to listen and involve others.

2. Explain that this activity is an opportunity for participants to practice giving active listening responses to statements they may hear in work-related situations.

3. Conduct a brief discussion in which you clarify the difference between hearing and listening. Mention that active listening is a two-way process that involves the following techniques:

   - Clarifying and confirming ("What I hear you saying is . . .")

- Reflecting underlying feelings ("I can imagine that you must feel . . .")
- Inviting further contribution ("Tell me more about . . .")

4. Distribute a copy of *Active Listening Responses* to each participant.

5. Ask them to work in pairs and write a response to each of the statements on the handout, and stress the importance of using one of the techniques you mentioned in step 3.

6. Tell them to use the words they would actually say so that their responses sound natural and conversational. Give them 10 minutes.

7. At the end of the 10 minutes, put each pair into a subgroup with one or two other pairs (for a total of four to six people), and ask them to share their responses with each other, making modifications to the statements where they feel it is appropriate.

8. Reconvene the entire group and ask subgroups to take turns sharing their responses with the others.

Discussion:

1. What was your reaction to developing the responses?

2. How were the responses different from those you may have given in similar situations?

3. How might these "new and improved" responses have an impact on the interaction between you and another person?

4. What are you going to do differently as a result of this activity?

Variations:

- If time is limited, you may choose to omit steps 7 and 8.
- You could have people work in pairs and practice responding to the statements verbally.

ACTIVE LISTENING RESPONSES WORKSHEET

Write an active listening response for each of the following statements. Be sure to use words that you would actually say.

1. I keep leaving voice mails, and no one returns my call. I don't know what else to do! I can't finish this project until I get the information from the other department.

2. I'm tired of doing other people's jobs, and they get all the credit.

3. Every time I ask him for help, he tells me to figure it out by myself.

4. There are so many changes going on around here. Just when I get used to one way of doing things, they change their mind and tell us to do something else.

5. These kids! They just don't have a good work ethic.

6. I know I told the customer about our return policy, but now she claims I didn't, and she is demanding a full refund.

7. It's getting harder and harder to attract and keep good employees.

ACTIVE OBSERVATION

Competency: Observing

Description: This activity is designed to help participants recognize the importance of observing as a leadership competency.

Goals:

- Heighten awareness of nonverbal communication.
- Improve personal observation skills.

Time Required: 30–40 minutes

Materials and Preparation:

- Select a 7- to 10-minute clip from a movie. Choose something that is obscure, such as a segment from a foreign film (without subtitles) or a very old movie to ensure that participants have not seen it. Keep in mind that any video you select is likely to be copyrighted and, therefore, you will need to have written permission from the work's owner. Here are some resources that will help you address the permissions issues and choose the right clips:

LinkedIn: MovEd—Movies in Education (online group). www.linkedin.com/groups/MovEd-Movies-in-Education-1944687.

Pluth, Becky Pike. (June 3, 2007). *101 Movie Clips That Teach and Train.* Pluth and Pluth.

Stim, Richard. (November 3, 2010). *Getting Permission: How to License and Clear Copyrighted Materials Online and Off.* NOLO.

- Appropriate video playback equipment.

Process:

1. Introduce the activity by explaining that you are going to show the participants a segment of a movie, and that you are deliberately turning off the sound.
2. Explain that they are to observe the actions and behaviors of the characters, and should be prepared to write a brief synopsis of what is taking place on the video. They are not to try to determine what the characters are saying, only what they think the nature of the interaction is. Their observations may include, but are not limited to, the atmosphere (hostile, friendly, romantic, tense, and so on); the

(Continued)

relationship between or among the characters; and what the characters might be discussing.

3. Show the video clip.

4. At the conclusion of the segment, ask the participants to work in pairs and write a brief description of what they think is happening in the video clip. Allow 3 to 4 minutes. Rewind the video while they are working on their synopses.

5. Ask for volunteers to share their responses with the entire group, including specific reasons for their conclusions. In other words, what was it about the characters' body language that suggested a certain conclusion?

6. After you have received several responses, play the video clip again, but this time include the audio as well.

Discussion:

1. How close were your interpretations to the actual situation?

2. If there were differences, what misled you? If you were close, what helped you?

3. How does this activity relate to anything you experience in the workplace?

4. What did you learn from the activity?

5. How can these insights help you in your interactions with others?

Variation:

- To avoid dealing with copyright issues, you could create your own video clip using friends, family members, or amateur actors.

Source: "Active Observation" by Karen Lawson in *SkillBuilders: 50 Communication Skills Activities.* Copyright © 2000 by HRDQ. Reproduced with permission.

COMMON GROUND

Competency: Managing Conflict

Description: This case study activity introduces participants to a structured process for helping others resolve conflict.

Goals:

- Follow a structured process for helping others resolve an interpersonal conflict.
- Apply the conflict resolution model to participants' own situations.

Time Required: 60–75 minutes

Materials and Preparation:

- *Guidelines for Helping Others Resolve Conflict* (one per participant)
- *Resolving Conflict* (one per participant)
- *Conflict Resolution Worksheet* (one per participant)
- *Case Study: Finding Common Ground* (one per participant)

Process:

1. Introduce the activity by explaining that sometimes leaders find themselves in the position of helping others resolve an interpersonal conflict.
2. Ask participants for examples of a situation in which they had to help mediate a conflict.
3. Also, ask them how difficult or easy it was for them in that role.
4. Explain that you are going to introduce them to a structured process for resolving conflict.
5. Distribute the *Guidelines for Helping Others Resolve Conflict* and review it with them. To illustrate and help them better understand "I statements," give them the following examples:
   - "I understand your position, but in my opinion . . ."
   - "I would prefer that . . ."
   - "I would like to find some way to reach an agreement that would satisfy both of us."
   - "I understand what you're saying, and although I don't agree with it entirely, I agree that . . . but disagree that . . ."
   - "Let's identify the things on which we can both agree."

(Continued)

6. Next, distribute the *Resolving Conflict* sheet and review the process with them, clarifying or further explaining as needed.

7. Tell them that they are now going to have an opportunity to apply the conflict resolution model to a case study. Distribute the *Conflict Resolution Worksheet* and *Case Study: Finding Common Ground*. Divide the group into subgroups of five to seven, and give them 20 minutes to complete the worksheet for the case study.

8. At the end of the 20 minutes, reconvene the entire group and solicit responses for each stage of the conflict resolution model they have identified. Then conduct a general discussion.

Discussion:

1. How realistic was the case study?
2. How helpful was the conflict resolution model?
3. How was this approach different from or similar to what you would normally have done in this situation?
4. How can you apply this model to your own situations?

Variation:

• In a multisession program, you may give this as an individual assignment between sessions.

GUIDELINES FOR HELPING OTHERS RESOLVE CONFLICT

As a leader you may find yourself in a position of helping others resolve an interpersonal conflict. Below are some guidelines to help you manage the conflict resolution process.

- Begin by establishing that the parties will be taking a collaborative approach to resolving the conflict, and that your role is to facilitate the process.
- Establish ground rules:
  - Use "I statements."
  - No personal attacks or accusations.
  - Don't interrupt.
- Manage the process and remain neutral.
- Ensure both parties listen to and understand each other.
- Encourage two-way discussion.
- Continue to focus on the goals for the conflict resolution process, not individual positions.
- Clarify and confirm throughout the process by asking each person to state what he or she heard the other person say.

Resolving Conflict

The following is a step-by-step process for resolving conflict.

Clarify and Define the Problem

- *Establish each person's agenda.* Each person states what he or she needs and wants.
- *Ensure each person understands the other's agenda.* Each person paraphrases the other's wants, needs, and position.

Establish Common Ground

- *Identify a common goal.* Each person states what he or she believes to be the desired outcome.
- *Search for areas of agreement.* The parties identify commonalities or points on which they both agree.
- *Identify areas of disagreement.* Each person states his or her perception of the points on which they disagree.
- *Seek to understand the other person's perspective, feelings, and so on.* Each person puts himself or herself "in the other person's shoes."

Generate Solution Options

- *Brainstorm possible solutions.* Both parties offer suggestions of acceptable alternatives.
- *Establish criteria to evaluate the options.* Both parties offer suggestions for evaluating the options.
- *Evaluate the options.* Both parties discuss the advantages and disadvantages of each option.

Reach a Resolution

- *Select an option.* Both parties agree on an option based on the discussion of the advantages and disadvantages of each option.
- *Develop an action plan.* Each person states what he or she is responsible for doing and specifies the specific steps he or she will take to resolve the problem.
- *Establish evaluation criteria.* Both parties determine how they will evaluate the success of the solution.
- *Evaluate the outcome.* Both parties will set a date to follow up and evaluate the outcome.

Conflict Resolution Worksheet

In your small group, refer to *Case Study: Finding Common Ground,* and for each step in the conflict resolution process write down the specific, open-ended questions you will ask or statements you will make to promote two-way discussion and elicit the desired outcome for that step.

Clarify and Define the Problem

- Establish each person's agenda.

- Ensure each person understands the other's agenda.

Establish Common Ground

- Identify a common goal.

- Search for areas of agreement.

- Identify areas of disagreement.

- Seek to understand the other person's perspective, feelings, and so on.

Generate Solution Options

- Brainstorm possible solutions.

- Establish criteria to evaluate the options.

- Evaluate the options.

Reach a Resolution

- Select an option.

- Develop an action plan.

- Establish evaluation criteria.

- Evaluate the outcome.

CASE STUDY: FINDING COMMON GROUND

One of the supervisors you oversee, Casey, is a long-term employee who has "come up through the ranks." Casey sets high standards and expectations for the department and its employees. Casey knows each job inside and out. He or she tends to take a hands-on approach to supervising and likes to know what's going on at all times. Casey is very thorough and detail-oriented, and wants to make sure he or she has all the information before making a decision.

Another one of the supervisors you oversee, Jordan, is a fairly new employee with considerable experience at another company. Jordan is enthusiastic, energetic, and self-motivated. Unlike Casey, Jordan tends to make decisions quickly, has no patience with time-consuming details, and just wants to get things done.

You have asked them to work on a special project to streamline order processing that involves both their departments. They have been working on the project for several weeks with little progress. They argue every time they get together to discuss the project, and each blames the other for the project's being behind schedule.

CONFLICTING AGENDAS

Competency: Managing Conflict

Description: This role-play activity gives participants an opportunity to practice helping two people to resolve a conflict.

Goals:

- Identify key behaviors critical to helping others resolve conflict.
- Use a structured process to help others resolve conflict.

Time Required: 90 minutes

Materials and Preparation:

- *Conflict Scenarios* (one per participant)
- *Resolving Conflict* from the Common Ground activity (one per participant)
- *Conflicting Agendas Observer Sheet* (one per participant)

Process:

1. Divide the group into subgroups of four participants each.
2. Explain that the purpose of this activity is to give the participants an opportunity to practice helping two people to resolve a conflict.
3. Distribute the three handouts (scenarios, model, and observer sheet) to all participants.
4. Tell them that they will engage in four role-play situations (10 minutes each), allowing them to experience the roles of mediating manager, employee, and observer. Point out that each person will twice play the role of an employee.
5. Give them 5 minutes to review the four scenarios.
6. Display the following schedule for the four role-play scenarios:

	Employee X	**Employee Y**	**Mediator**	**Observer**
Round 1	A	B	C	D
Round 2	B	C	D	A
Round 3	C	D	A	B
Round 4	D	A	B	C

7. Ask members of the subgroups to decide which role each person will take in each round by labeling themselves A, B, C, and D and following the schedule from step 6. Give them 5 minutes to review their assignments for Round 1.

(Continued)

8. Begin Round 1, and give participants 10 minutes.

9. Call time after 10 minutes and ask the subgroups to spend 5 minutes discussing the interaction and getting feedback from the observer.

10. Repeat the process for Rounds 2, 3, and 4.

11. At the end of the Round 4 discussion, reconvene the entire group and conduct a general discussion.

Discussion:

1. What was your reaction to the role-play activity?

2. How difficult was it to apply the model or process to the situation?

3. What was your reaction when you were in the role of an employee?

4. What insights did you gain from this activity?

5. How was this approach similar to or different from what you would have done in a comparable situation?

6. How can this help you in your role as a leader when you need to help others resolve conflict?

Variations:

• Rather than using the prepared role-play situations, participants may submit their own role-play scenarios prior to the session.

• If time is limited, you may limit the number of role-play scenarios and allow subgroup members to choose the ones most appropriate for them.

CONFLICT SCENARIOS

In your subgroup, rotate the roles of the two employees in conflict, the mediator, and the observer for each round.

ROUND 1: SHARING RESOURCES

Two managers share an assistant for two respective projects. From the beginning of the arrangement, the two disagreed as to how the assistant's time and workload should be split. Manager A believes he or she is not getting adequate support from the assistant because Manager B is assigning so much work to the assistant that there is little time for the assistant to devote to Manager A's project. Also, Manager B complains about the assistant's performance and gives the assistant a poor rating on the assistant's performance appraisal. Manager A, however, is quite happy with the assistant's performance and believes Manager B's assessment is inaccurate and unfair. Each complains to you about the other.

ROUND 2: DIFFERING VIEWPOINTS

Two employees on the same team do not get along. Each complains to you about the other. Each accuses the other of "slacking off" and being difficult to work with. It has gotten to the point where the two people try to avoid each other as much as possible. Although both employees have told you they can't stand working with the other, they have asked you not to say anything.

ROUND 3: GETTING ALONG

The administrative assistant (AA) for your sales team does an excellent job—he or she is experienced, knows the customers, and has strong office organization skills. The AA has told you he or she is having trouble getting along with a particular account executive (AE). The AE tends to be demanding, "telling" the AA what he or she needs instead of "asking" for her help. The AE also gives the AA a lot of last-minute "urgent" requests and doesn't thank the AA for the work he or she does for the AE. The AA has asked you to assign the AE to another sales team so he or she doesn't have to work with this particular AE. When you asked the AE about the situation, the AE said he or she doesn't understand the problem, and it's up to the AA to give the AE the support he or she needs. You are not going

(Continued)

to reassign either of them to another team, but now they're avoiding each other and complaining about the other to the rest of the team.

ROUND 4: TO SPEND OR NOT TO SPEND?

Two senior managers disagree about installing a new, costly state-of-the art computer system. Manager A is young and innovative, and believes that an upgrade is necessary in order to maintain workplace efficiency and keep up with the competition. Manager B tends to be more fiscally conservative and believes an upgrade at this time is unwarranted due to uncertain economic conditions and the desire to prevent any employee layoffs. Each comes to you complaining about the other.

CONFLICTING AGENDAS OBSERVER SHEET

As you observe the role-play, note how well the mediating manager facilitates the conflict resolution process. Please be as specific as possible.

A. How well did the mediating manager help the two people . . .

1. Establish their individual agendas?

2. Ensure they understand each other's agenda?

3. Identify a common goal?

4. Identify areas of agreement and disagreement?

5. Understand each other's perspective, feelings, position, and so on?

6. Identify possible solutions?

7. Establish criteria to evaluate the options?

8. Discuss the advantages and disadvantages of each option?

9. Select an option that is acceptable to both?

10. Develop an action plan with clear roles, responsibilities, and so on?

11. Establish a way to evaluate the success of the resolution?

B. How well did the manager facilitate the process by . . .

1. Remaining neutral?

2. Encouraging two-way discussion?

3. Establishing and "enforcing" ground rules?

4. Keeping the discussion focused on the common goal?

GIVING FEEDBACK

Competency: Giving Feedback

Description: This self-assessment activity gives participants an opportunity to assess their effectiveness in providing feedback to others.

Goals:

- Assess participants' effectiveness in providing feedback to others.
- Explain the importance of giving feedback to employees on a regular basis.

Time Required: 20–30 minutes

Materials and Preparation:

- *Giving Feedback Self-Assessment* (one per participant)

Process:

1. Introduce the activity by explaining that being able to give constructive feedback to others is an important interpersonal skill that effective leaders have mastered. Emphasize that the purpose of giving feedback is to help the other person; it should not be used criticize or tear down. It must be constructive, not destructive; it should be intended to inform; and it ought to be delivered with genuine care and concern. Feedback is fundamental to developing and maintaining relationships.

2. Ask participants to share examples of situations in which they may choose to give feedback to another person. Emphasize that giving feedback is not limited to their employees. Sometimes they may need to give feedback to their colleagues, their bosses, or even their customers.

3. Then ask them to indicate by a show of hands if they think they do a good job of giving feedback.

4. Explain that you are going to give them an opportunity to assess how well they provide feedback.

5. Distribute the *Giving Feedback Self-Assessment* to the participants and ask them to complete it, stressing that their responses should reflect their behavior in most situations. Give them 10 minutes to complete the assessment and score it.

6. At the end of the 10 minutes, reconvene the entire group to conduct a general discussion.

Discussion:

1. What was your reaction to your self-assessment? How did you feel about completing it?
2. On what specific items did you give yourself a low score?
3. What did you learn about your own approach to giving feedback?
4. What insights did you gain, and how can these be helpful to you both professionally and personally?
5. What might you do differently when giving feedback in the future?

Variations:

- If time permits, you may choose to have people work in pairs to discuss their assessments with each other prior to the large-group discussion.
- This assessment can be used in a one-on-one coaching situation.
- You may ask participants to complete the self-assessment prior to the session.

Giving Feedback Self-Assessment

Using the following key, indicate to what degree each of the following statements is characteristic of your actions or behavior.

5 = Almost always (over 80 percent of the time); 4 = Often (61 to 80 percent of the time); 3 = Sometimes (41 to 60 percent of the time); 2 = Seldom (20 to 40 percent of the time); 1 = Almost never (less than 20 percent of the time)

When giving feedback to someone, I . . .

_____ 1. Genuinely want to help the other person

_____ 2. Make sure the behavior is something the person can change

_____ 3. Try to deliver my message immediately or as close to the incident as possible

_____ 4. Remove any physical barrier (such as a desk or table) that may inhibit our discussion

_____ 5. Check to see if the feedback is wanted, or at least give the person an opportunity to have input as to when the discussion will take place

_____ 6. Avoid speculating or making assumptions about the person's motivations or intentions in regard to his or her behavior

_____ 7. Describe behavior that can be observed or measured—that is, specifically what the person did or said

_____ 8. Describe observable behavior in the context of specific incidents or situations

_____ 9. Avoid using evaluative or judgmental words, such as "good," "bad," "poor," or "excellent"

_____ 10. Provide specific examples or concrete details of the person's behavior

_____ 11. Include a statement about my feelings or reaction to the person's behavior

_____ 12. State clearly what I want the person to do differently

_____ 13. Point out the positive consequences or benefits of the behavior change as prompted by the feedback

_____ 14. Ask the individual to explain his or her understanding of the situation

_____ 15. Ask the individual what he or she is going to do to change behavior or improve the situation

Scoring: To find your overall score, simply add together the values you have given for the items above. Then refer to the following interpretation:

70–75	You have mastered the art of giving feedback. You can be a good role model and coach for others.
60–69	You demonstrate many competent behaviors; however, there is still room for improvement. Concentrate on fine-tuning your approach.
38–59	Your feedback skills need some work. Share your approach with someone whose opinion you respect, and ask for feedback yourself.
21–37	You still have a lot to learn about giving feedback. Review your responses and identify key areas for improvement.
15–20	Your approach to giving feedback could do more harm than good. Seek out a competent coach to help you improve your feedback skills.

LISTENING SELF-AWARENESS ASSESSMENT

Competency: Listening

Description: The purpose of this activity is to help participants identify effective listening skills and assess how well they practice them.

Goals:

- Assess participants' listening habits.
- Develop an action plan to improve listening skills.

Time Required: 20–30 minutes

Materials and Preparation:

- *Listening Self-Awareness Assessment* (one per participant)
- *Listening Self-Awareness Worksheet* (one per participant)

Process:

1. Distribute one copy of the *Listening Self-Awareness Assessment* to each participant.
2. Explain that you want them to think about their current listening behaviors and habits and respond to each item in the assessment by using check marks to indicate how frequently they practice a particular behavior. Allow approximately 8 minutes for them to complete the assessment.
3. After the participants have completed the assessment, ask them to choose two to three items for improvement.
4. Divide the group into subgroups of four to five. Distribute a copy of the *Listening Self-Awareness Worksheet* to each participant and have them write down the listening behaviors they want to improve.
5. Using the following model, ask the participants to take turns sharing their items for improvement while the other members of the subgroup offer suggestions on how each person can improve. Allow 3 minutes per person.
   - The participant identifies one listening barrier, stating what he or she wants to improve ("I would like to do a better job of . . .").
   - Each subgroup member gives that person a piece of advice.
   - The participant says, "Thank you."
   - The subgroup moves on to someone else.
6. Instruct the participants to record the suggestions from their colleagues on the *Listening Self-Awareness Worksheet.*

7. After everyone has had an opportunity to receive suggestions from his or her colleagues, ask a spokesperson from each subgroup to choose one example of an item for improvement and its corresponding suggestions and share it with the entire group.

Discussion:
1. What was your reaction to the activity?
2. What did you learn about yourself?
3. How helpful was the advice you received from your colleagues?
4. How are you going to use the advice in your interactions with others?

Variations:
- Instead of forming subgroups, you can choose to have participants work in pairs.
- After the participants have recorded their suggestions from their colleagues, ask them to identify one or two items for improvement and develop an action plan to improve those behaviors. Then have them share their action items with their subgroup.

LISTENING SELF-AWARENESS ASSESSMENT

Think about your one-on-one interactions on the job. For each item below, indicate how frequently you practice a particular behavior by placing a check mark in the appropriate box.

	Almost Always (over 80%)	Often (61%–80%)	Sometimes (41%–60%)	Seldom (20%–40%)	Almost Never (less than 20%)
1. I maintain eye contact with the speaker.					
2. I allow the other person to finish speaking before I respond.					
3. I refrain from doing other things while the person is speaking.					
4. I refrain from forming a rebuttal in my head while the person is speaking.					
5. I ask open-ended questions to clarify my understanding.					
6. I observe nonverbal cues (such as facial expressions and body language) that contradict or support the other person's message.					
7. I paraphrase what I think the other person has said to ensure my understanding of his or her message.					
8. I use nonverbal cues (such as head nodding and leaning forward) to encourage the person to continue.					
9. I focus on what the other person is saying even if I'm not interested or disagree with the message.					
10. I take notes to capture the main ideas of the conversation.					

11. I use interjections (*uh-huh, right, go on, tell me more*) to encourage the person to expand on his or her comments.					
12. I listen for the tone as well as the words.					
13. I refrain from thinking of other things while the other person is talking.					
14. I try to identify the speaker's central ideas or main message.					
15. I try to see things from the speaker's perspective— that is, "where he or she is coming from."					
16. I try not to become defensive or overreact to emotionally charged words.					
17. I offer a summary of the speaker's main ideas at the end of the conversation.					
18. I understand that words may mean different things to different people.					
19. I think about how the other person may react to what I say before I respond.					
20. I am aware of how my tone or body language may intimidate the other person.					
21. I confirm my perception of the speaker's feelings by acknowledging the emotion he or she might be experiencing.					

Scoring: Tally each column. Multiply each column as noted in the following scale—that is, multiply the "almost always" column by 5, "often" by 4, and so on.

Column	Number of Checks	×	Rating Value	=	Total
Almost always		×	5	=	
Often		×	4	=	
Sometimes		×	3	=	
Seldom		×	2	=	
Almost never		×	1	=	
				Total Score:	

(*Continued*)

Once you have the number for each of the separate columns, add all of the numbers together to get your total score. Please refer to the categories and their point values to interpret your score:

92–100	**Effective active listener**
	You excel in promoting two-way communication and understanding.
75–91	**Inconsistent active listener**
	You miss some key opportunities to involve others in the communication process.
46–74	**Developing active listener**
	Although you have some basic knowledge of active listening, you need to consciously work to improve your listening skills.
29–45	**Struggling active listener**
	Your current listening habits may have a negative impact on your interactions with others.
20–28	**Ineffective active listener**
	Your active listening skills need a lot of work.

LISTENING SELF-AWARENESS WORKSHEET

Identify the listening behaviors you want to improve, and record the suggestions from your colleagues. Then create an action plan, indicating what you are going to do to improve your listening behaviors, being as specific as possible.

Item 1:
Suggestions:

Item 2:
Suggestions:

Item 3:
Suggestions:

Action Plan:

MIXED MESSAGES

Competencies: Communicating, Congruence, Listening

Description: In this activity, participants explore the dynamics of the three elements (verbal, vocal, and visual) of communication.

Goals:

- Identify the importance of congruence among verbal, vocal, and visual elements of communication.
- Recognize how the three elements of communication can have an impact on the communication process.

Time Required: 50–60 minutes

Materials and Preparation:

- Flip chart page with the following schedule:

	Speaker	**Listener**	**Observer**
Round 1	A	B	C
Round 2	B	C	A
Round 3	C	A	B

- *Observer's Worksheet* (one per participant).
- *Listener Roles*
  - *Listener: Round 1* (one per trio)
  - *Listener: Round 2* (one per trio)
  - *Listener: Round 3* (one per trio)
- *Speaker Roles*
  - *Speaker: Round 1* (one per trio)
  - *Speaker: Round 2* (one per trio)
  - *Speaker: Round 3* (one per trio)

Process:

1. Introduce the activity by explaining that participants will have an opportunity to discuss communication problems within their organization. Specifically, they will discuss the following three questions:
   - What are some examples of communication problems within your organization?

- What are some possible causes of the communication problems within this organization?
- What specific suggestions do you have for solving the communication problems within the organization?

2. Divide the group into subgroups of three. Explain that the interaction will consist of three rounds, and that they will have an opportunity to play each of the three roles: speaker, listener, and observer. They will rotate the roles in each of the three rounds.

3. Ask members of each trio to identify themselves as A, B, or C. Call their attention to the schedule posted on the flip chart, and mention that each round will be 7 minutes.

4. Distribute the *Observer's Worksheet* and tell participants that the observers are to complete the worksheet for each round. Also let them know that the speakers and listeners will receive their roles at the beginning of the round, and that the instructions are self-explanatory. Tell them that they are not to share the information on the instruction sheets.

5. Distribute Round 1 listener and speaker roles. Remind the observers to take notes as they study the interaction. After all participants have reviewed their instructions, begin Round 1. Give them 7 minutes.

6. At the end of the 7 minutes, call time and repeat the process for Round 2 and Round 3.

7. At the end of Round 3, reconvene the entire group and ask the observers to share their observations of each round, particularly focusing on the effects of the listener's behavior on the speaker.

8. Explain that three elements are present in any one-on-one, face-to-face interaction:
   Verbal—what we say (words)
   Vocal—how we say it (tone)
   Visual—how we show it (body language)

9. Ask the entire group to discuss the impact of each element on the communication process they just experienced.

10. Emphasize that all three elements must be congruent. Congruent messages are those in which the nonverbal elements match or reinforce the verbal message. Ask for workplace examples in which the verbal and nonverbal elements are not congruent. (For example, the manager says, "I'm listening" to an employee but at the same time

(Continued)

continues to read e-mails or engage in some other activity while the employee is trying to have a conversation.)

Discussion:
1. How did you feel in your role as a speaker? As a listener?
2. How was this experience similar to or different from your experiences at work?
3. What did you learn about the impact of the vocal and visual elements on communication?
4. How does this relate to your role as a leader?
5. What might you do differently as a result of this activity?

Variations:
- If you are short on time and you have at least three trios, you may choose to have only one round and assign each trio a different listener role. In that case, the speaker would address only the Round 1 question.
- You could ask the observers to give feedback to the speakers and listeners after each round instead of waiting until all three rounds have been completed.

Observer's Worksheet

Observe carefully the interaction between the speaker and the listener. Note the specific behavior of the listener and then the speaker's reaction. Be sure to document the verbal and the nonverbal reactions of both people.

	Listener's Behavior	**Speaker's Reaction**
Eye contact		
Gestures		
Posture and body position		
Other nonverbal behavior		
Tone of voice		
Word choice		

LISTENER ROLES

LISTENER: ROUND 1

- Pretend to listen.
- Look away from the speaker while he or she is talking.
- Do other things, such as doodle or use your electronic handheld device.
- Slump in your chair.
- Make sure your tone of voice reflects disinterest.

LISTENER: ROUND 2

- Maintain eye contact.
- Pretend to be attentive although you may be thinking of something else.
- Smile throughout the conversation.
- Agree with everything the speaker says, even if you have a different opinion or viewpoint.
- If the speaker asks you a question, give a brief, noncommittal response.

LISTENER: ROUND 3

- Maintain direct eye contact.
- Clarify and confirm your understanding of what the speaker is saying.
- Encourage further contribution.
- Indicate interest through nonverbal signals, such as leaning forward.
- Ask open-ended questions.
- Use a pleasant and genuine tone of voice.

SPEAKER ROLES

SPEAKER: ROUND 1

Discuss with your partner examples of communication problems within your organization. These problem areas might include methods of communication (e-mails, phone calls, face-to-face meetings, and so on); flow of information (for example, between managers and employees or between and among departments); or anything else relating to poor communication. Solicit your partner's opinion and ideas.

SPEAKER: ROUND 2

Discuss with your partner some possible causes of the communication problems within your organization (for example, nonexistent or infrequent staff meetings, lack of accountability). Solicit your partner's opinion and ideas.

SPEAKER: ROUND 3

Discuss with your partner your suggestions for solving communication problems within the organization. Solicit your partner's ideas as well.

PICTURE THIS

Competency: Observing

Description: This activity is designed to help participants identify how well they observe and pay attention to detail by looking at two pictures of the same thing and trying to find the differences between the two pictures.

Goals:

- Improve participants' powers of observation.
- Recognize strengths and shortcomings of participants' ability to observe visual cues.
- Identify the importance of observing as a leadership competency.

Time Required: 30–45 minutes

Materials and Preparation:

- Purchase one or more of the picture puzzle books published by *Life Magazine*. Each page has two pictures of the same thing; however, the second picture has been altered.
- Tear out the pictures and laminate them so you may reuse them. Plan on one picture per participant.
- Choose pictures that have the same number of alterations (generally six or eight).
- Prepare an answer key for each picture puzzle.
- To make it easier to distribute and keep track of the picture puzzles and the answer keys, number each one.
- Have ready a flip chart page or slide with the following questions:
  - Give examples of visual cues you have noticed (or missed) in your work environment, particularly as they relate to employees.
  - What was the significance or impact of these visual cues?
  - How do a person's powers of observation influence his or her success as a leader?

Process:

1. Introduce the activity by stating that observing is an important leadership competency.
2. Ask participants each to raise their hand if they think they have good observation skills.
3. Explain that they will have an opportunity to "test" their powers of observation by looking at two pictures of the same thing and spotting the alterations in the second picture.

4. Distribute the pictures facedown to each participant and ask participants not to look at them until you give the signal.

5. After each person has received two pictures, tell them they may turn the pictures over and that they have 10 minutes to find the differences between the two pictures and write down their answers.

6. At the end of the 10 minutes, call time and distribute the appropriate answer key to each participant. Ask them to check their answers against the answer key.

7. Ask the participants how well they did—that is, how many alterations they identified.

8. Form subgroups of four or five and ask them to spend 10 minutes discussing the following questions displayed on a flip chart page or slide:
   - Give examples of visual cues you have noticed (or missed) in your work environment, particularly as they relate to employees.
   - What was the significance or impact of these visual cues?
   - How do a person's powers of observation influence his or her success as a leader?

9. Reconvene the entire group and ask participants to summarize their discussions.

Discussion:

1. What was your reaction to having to identify the picture alterations within a specific time limit?

2. How is this similar to what you have experienced in your work environment?

3. What did you learn about yourself through this activity?

4. What can you do differently to improve your observation skills?

Variations:

- You may choose to make this an individual or team competition and award prizes. For a team competition, put people in teams of four or five. Each person will still have an individual puzzle to solve; however, the team members will combine (or average) their individual scores, and prizes will be awarded to the winning team.

- Depending on time constraints, you may choose to have more than one round of puzzles to solve.

THE ART OF ASKING QUESTIONS

Competency: Communicating, Questioning

Description: The purpose of this activity is to help participants recognize the importance of asking rather than telling in their roles as leaders.

Goals:

* Distinguish between open-ended and closed-ended questions.
* Ask open-ended questions to gain a better understanding of the people with whom participants are having a conversation.
* Identify the value of asking open-ended questions

Time Required: 30 minutes

Materials and Preparation:

* Slide or flip chart page showing the following questions:
  * Do you understand?
  * Do you have any questions?
* Slide or flip chart page showing the following questions:
  * What is your understanding of . . . ?
  * What questions do you have?
* *Asking the Right Questions Worksheet* (one per participant)

Process:

1. Introduce the activity by explaining that effective leaders ask rather than tell. In the past, leaders tended to dictate, give orders, and simply tell people what to do rather than inquire. Today's leaders ask the right questions to help people find solutions themselves and increase their self-confidence. In addition to their use in problem solving, questioning techniques are effective in situations involving coaching and stimulating creativity. Emphasize that powerful questions begin with "what" and "how," and that leaders should avoid asking questions that begin with "why" because they put people on the defensive. Also, note that leaders must be careful not to unleash a barrage of questions that could sound like interrogation.

2. Demonstrate the difference between an open-ended and a closed-ended question by showing a slide or flip chart page with the following closed-ended questions:
   * Do you understand?
   * Do you have any questions?

3. Ask people to indicate by a show of hands if they ever use these questions. Point out that these questions are answerable by "yes" or "no" and offer no real insight. Solicit from the group how they could make these two questions open-ended, and then show the following:

   • What is your understanding of . . . ?
   • What questions do you have?

4. Conduct a brief discussion as to the reason these open-ended questions are more effective.

5. Next, explain that participants will have an opportunity to practice turning closed-ended questions into open-ended questions.

6. Distribute the *Asking the Right Questions Worksheet.*

7. Ask people to work in pairs to complete the worksheet. Give them 8 minutes.

8. At the end of the 8 minutes, reconvene the entire group and ask for volunteers to share their responses.

Discussion:

1. What was your reaction to creating open-ended questions?

2. What did you learn from this activity?

3. How can asking open-ended questions help you become more effective as a leader?

Variation:

• Put people in pairs to practice asking and responding to the open-ended questions generated in Part Two of the worksheet.

The Art of Asking Questions Worksheet

Part One: Rewrite each of the following questions so that it is open-ended and encourages two-way, open communication.

1. Why didn't you tell me about your time constraints?

2. How can you say this approach won't work?

3. Isn't it true that cost cutting is the number one priority?

4. Do you honestly think we should move ahead on this project?

5. Is it fair to say that the cost for the proposed system is high?

Part Two: Develop an open-ended question ("how" or "what") that will elicit the type of response you desire from the other person.

1. Get the person to take ownership of his or her behavior.

2. Inspire the person to engage in breakthrough thinking.

3. Encourage the person to see the situation differently.

4. Make sure the person understands your request.

5. Uncover the person's reason for making a specific decision.

6. Identify the person's challenges in completing an assignment.

THE ART OF INFLUENCING

Competency: Influencing

Description: In this activity, participants explore the importance of using influencing skills to gain commitment from others or to motivate them to do what they want them to do.

Goals:

- Explain the concept and importance of influencing.
- Identify the skills and techniques used in influencing others.

Time Required: 45 minutes

Materials and Preparation:

- Flip chart pages
- Markers

Process:

1. Introduce the activity by explaining that effective leaders are masters of influencing. The key to influencing is connecting with the people we want to influence. Master influencers connect with people by understanding their perspectives and addressing their problems, hopes, fears, and dreams.

2. Discuss briefly the difference between compliance and commitment. Compliance implies that people will do what you want them to do because they "have to." Point out that effective leaders gain commitment from others by identifying and tapping into others' WIIFM (What's In It For Me?).

3. Solicit from the group examples of topics and situations in the context of which they would like to persuade or influence an individual or group. Post these on a flip chart page. Examples may include the following:

   - Working longer hours
   - Cutting expenses and operating costs
   - Implementing a new procedure
   - Embracing a new technology
   - Donating money to a cause
   - Accepting a new policy

4. To illustrate the approach one might use to connect with and influence someone else, solicit from the group (or suggest yourself) a family-related scenario, such as engaging

(Continued)

in a family activity, breaking a family tradition, or moving to a new area. Use the following questions to guide the activity:

- What is the situation or scenario?
- How would each of the family members feel about the proposed plan?
- What might be the causes of resistance (fears, problems, and so on)?
- What might be the disadvantages to each person involved?
- What might be the benefits to each person?
- Based on your analysis and understanding of each person's perspective, how would you "sell" the idea to each family member?

5. After the group has worked through the sample scenario, divide the group into subgroups of four or five and assign each group a different situation or scenario based on examples generated earlier. Ask them to discuss how they would approach the situation, using the same questions used in the large-group exercise. Give them 15 minutes.

6. At the end of the 15 minutes, reconvene the group and solicit their examples.

Discussion:

1. How was this approach different from or similar to the approach you would normally use?
2. How effective was this approach?
3. How can you use this approach in future situations?

Variation:

- Rather than work-related situations, ask the participants to choose community-related examples.
- Ask the subgroups to role-play their approaches to influencing.

WHAT DO YOU MEAN?

Competency: Communicating

Description: This activity shows how words mean different things to different people, and how misinterpretations of these common words can lead to misunderstandings and even conflict.

Goals:

- Identify the importance of being specific.

Time Required: 20 minutes

Materials and Preparation:

- Flip chart page displaying the phrases that appear on the *What Do You Mean? Worksheet*
- *What Do You Mean? Worksheet* (one per participant)
- Blank flip chart pages
- Markers

Process:

1. Distribute a copy of the *What Do You Mean? Worksheet* to each participant.

2. Ask the participants to complete the worksheet by reading each statement and then answering the question following that statement. Point out that in answering the questions, they need to provide specific numbers, percentages, time frames, and so on. Also mention that you are looking for what *they think* the statements mean, and that they shouldn't spend time trying to analyze them. Give them 5 minutes.

3. After they have completed the worksheet, solicit responses and record them on the flip chart. If the group is twelve or fewer, you can go around the room and quickly record each person's response. For a group larger than twelve, you might solicit responses from people picked at random.

4. After soliciting and recording the responses, ask the participants what they notice in the different responses. (The responses will probably vary considerably.)

5. Choose four or five of the statements and ask participants to suggest ways to make them more precise.

6. Point out that participants should avoid using such inexact words when delivering their own messages. Also mention that if they are on the receiving end of these unclear messages, they should ask the sender to be more specific.

(Continued)

Discussion:

1. What was your reaction to the activity?
2. How is this similar to what you have experienced in the workplace? Give specific examples.
3. What is the key learning point of this activity?
4. What will you do differently as a result of this activity?

Variations:

- If time is limited, you may assign one or two items from the *What Do You Mean? Worksheet* to each person, instead of asking everyone to complete all ten.
- If time permits, you may want to put people in pairs and have them role-play how they would respond to the inexact messages in order to gain clarification.

WHAT DO YOU MEAN? WORKSHEET

For each of the following statements, answer the question that follows the statement.

1. Please send the report **as soon as possible.** (What is the deadline for the report?)

2. It is very difficult to train **older** workers. (How old are the workers?)

3. I want you to come to work **early** tomorrow. (What time should you come to work?)

4. We have gotten complaints from **a lot** of customers. (How many customers have complained?)

5. John **usually** completes his work on time. (What percentage of John's work is completed on time?)

6. Please sign the enclosed contract and return it **at your earliest convenience.** (When does the person expect to receive it?)

7. I have given you **several** opportunities to meet the deadline. (How many opportunities did you give?)

8. I'll need some additional **time** to prepare my report. (How much time do you need?)

9. This project will take a **while** to complete. (How long will it take?)

10. I anticipate a **large** group will be attending the program. (How many people are in the group?)

CHAPTER SIX

MOTIVATING AND ENGAGING

This chapter presents activities to help leaders create an environment in which people are engaged and are motivated to do their best. These activities address the skills that leaders must employ and practice to promote a positive motivational climate.

EMBRACING CHANGE

Competency: Leading Change

Description: The purpose of this activity is to help participants identify what they can do , to bring about positive change for themselves as well as for their organization.

Goals:

- Identify participants' roles as change agents.
- Identify ways to positively influence change in an organization.

Time Required: 30 minutes

Materials and Preparation:

- Flip chart pages with one of the following questions on each:
  - What changes are going on in your organization or department right now?
  - What can **others do** so that you can feel more comfortable with the change or changes?
  - What can **you do** so that you are more comfortable with the change or changes?
  - What opportunities may come out of the change or changes?
- Blank flip chart pages
- Markers
- Masking tape

Process:

1. Post the following question on a flip chart page: "What changes are going on in your organization and department right now?"
2. Solicit input from the group and capture the changes on the flip chart page. Identify one or two specific changes as topics for discussion.
3. Ask the group the following question: "How do you feel about this change (or these changes)?" Capture the comments on a flip chart page.
4. Divide the group into subgroups of four or five people. If you have only one topic, all subgroups will address the topic. If you have identified two topics, then assign a different topic to each subgroup.
5. Post the following questions:
   - What can **others do** so that you can feel more comfortable with the change or changes?
   - What can **you do** so that you are more comfortable with the change or changes?
   - What opportunities may come out of the change or changes?

6. Ask each subgroup to discuss each question and select a spokesperson to represent the subgroup. Give them 15 minutes.

7. At the end of the designated period, solicit input and post the ideas and suggestions on flip chart pages.

Discussion:

1. What was your reaction to the activity?

2. What did you learn from the activity?

3. What can you do to make change work in your organization?

Variation:

• Instead of asking the participants to identify changes, you may choose to focus on a change of your choice.

EMPOWERING OTHERS

Competency: Empowering

Description: This self-assessment activity is designed to give participants the opportunity to reflect on the degree to which they empower their employees.

Goals:

- Assess participants' empowerment behaviors.
- Identify ways a leader can empower employees.

Time Required: 45 minutes

Materials and Preparation:

- *Employee Empowerment Checklist* (one per participant)

Process:

1. Introduce the activity by explaining that empowered employees are engaged employees, and engaged employees are more committed and involved in their organization and less likely to leave.

2. Ask participants what they think the word *empowerment* means. Solicit responses, and then offer the following explanation: "Empowerment means making people feel valued by involving them in decisions, incorporating their ideas, asking them to participate in the planning process, praising them, and recognizing and rewarding them for their achievements and efforts."

3. Ask participants by a show of hands to indicate if they think they do a good job of empowering their employees. Ask them to share specific examples.

4. Tell them that you are going to give them an opportunity to examine their own employee empowerment behaviors.

5. Distribute the *Employee Empowerment Checklist* and ask them to take a few minutes and respond by checking "yes" or "no." Give them 10 minutes.

6. At the end of the 10 minutes, create subgroups of five to seven people and ask them to compare their checklist responses, particularly noting those for which they checked "yes," and to share specific examples of what they do that illustrates that behavior. Instruct the participants to capture ideas they can use with their own employees. Give them 15 minutes.

7. At the end of the 15 minutes, reconvene the entire group and conduct a general discussion.

Discussion:
1. What did you learn about yourself through this self-assessment?
2. On what particular items did you check "no"?
3. What specific ideas did you gain from your colleagues?
4. What are some ways you can create a culture of empowerment?

Variation:
• If time is limited, you may choose to eliminate the subgroup activity and just focus on the insights participants gained from their responses to the checklist.

EMPLOYEE EMPOWERMENT CHECKLIST

For each of the following statements, check "yes" or "no" to indicate whether or not you practice that behavior on a regular basis.

Do you . . .

	Yes	No
1. Inform employees of all data relative to their jobs as well as to the goals and direction of the organization?	☐	☐
2. Involve your employees in determining their organization's goals?	☐	☐
3. Explain to employees how what they do fits into the "big picture"?	☐	☐
4. Give people the training and resources they need to do their job?	☐	☐
5. Set boundaries rather than establish strict rules and procedures?	☐	☐
6. Give specific and frequent feedback to employees on their performance?	☐	☐
7. Communicate clear expectations and standards of performance?	☐	☐
8. Express confidence in your employees' ability to do their job?	☐	☐
9. Encourage employees to suggest new ideas or better ways doing things?	☐	☐
10. Hold people accountable for their decisions and actions?	☐	☐
11. Help employees develop the competencies they need to handle additional power, responsibility, and authority?	☐	☐
12. Encourage employees to think for themselves and find creative ways to solve problems and get the job done?	☐	☐
13. Communicate that asking for support and assistance is a sign of strength, not weakness?	☐	☐
14. Reward employees who take the initiative and "go the extra mile"?	☐	☐
15. Trust employees to do things right?	☐	☐
16. Encourage employees to make decisions about how to do their work?	☐	☐
17. Involve employees in decisions that affect them?	☐	☐
18. Ask employees for input in planning changes?	☐	☐
19. Allow employees to set their own goals?	☐	☐
20. Encourage employees to use good judgment in all situations?	☐	☐
21. Encourage employees to take risks based on sound judgment?	☐	☐

22. Use mistakes or errors in judgment as opportunities for coaching rather than punishing? ☐ ☐
23. Encourage employees to take the initiative in seeking information and resources across department lines rather than adhering to a rigid chain of command? ☐ ☐
24. Create a climate of trust, openness, and acceptance? ☐ ☐

FAIR OR EQUAL?

Competency: Fairness

Description: In this case study activity, participants will examine the difference between treating people fairly and treating people equally. They will also discuss how employees may perceive a leader's behavior.

Goals:

- Distinguish between treating people fairly and treating them equally.
- Recognize the importance of consistency in a leader's behavior toward employees.

Time Required: 45–60 minutes

Materials and Preparation:

- *Case Study: Fair or Equal?* (one per participant)

Process:

1. Introduce the activity by explaining that effective leaders are both fair and consistent. Point out that if they are perceived otherwise, the result is low morale and poor performance. Explain further that it is not always easy to be fair, even if you try to be.
2. Divide the group into subgroups of five to seven and distribute copies of *Case Study: Fair or Equal?* Ask participants to read the case study individually and answer the discussion questions. Give them about 10 minutes.
3. At the end of the time period, ask them to discuss the case in their subgroups using the questions to guide their discussion. Give them 20 minutes.
4. At the end of the 20 minutes, reconvene the entire group and ask for their reactions to the discussion questions.

Discussion:

1. What are some examples of other situations in which a manager has seemingly been unfair to someone? What was the impact on the individual as well as the other employees?
2. How does consistency relate to treating people fairly and treating people equally?
3. What can you do to ensure fairness and consistency with your employees?

Variation:

- Instead of using this as a case study, you can introduce the scenario and ask the participants to role-play in trios, with each group member assuming the role of Dana, Payton, or the manager.

CASE STUDY: FAIR OR EQUAL?

You are the manager of a ten-person department. Like most other departments in the organization, your group is feeling the pressure of doing more with fewer people. Your group members range in age from late twenties to early forties, and most of them have been in the department less than two years. Some have only been there a few months. Two of your employees, Dana and Payton, both senior members of the department, are working on a special project with a tight deadline. As senior members, they informally supervise the less experienced team members.

Payton is a single parent of two small children and has made special arrangements with you to come in every day an hour early so he or she can take Friday off (child care is not available on Fridays). Payton is very conscientious and makes sure his or her work is complete before leaving each day.

Dana is also a hardworking employee who puts in long hours and sometimes voluntarily works weekends (without being paid overtime) so that the project stays on schedule. Dana approaches you on Monday and asks to take Friday off in order to chaperone his or her child's school field trip. You mention that it is very important that either Dana or Payton is at work on Friday due to the critical nature of the project and the lack of experienced team members. Dana reacts by saying, "I don't understand why I can't take just one Friday off, especially when Payton gets every Friday off. I put in a lot of extra hours, including weekends, and don't complain. This is very important to me. I think it's only fair that I be able to take off on a Friday every once in a while."

Discussion Questions

1. What is your reaction to the manager's response to Dana?
2. What is your reaction to Payton's work arrangement?
3. What happens if the manager is not perceived as being fair?
4. What does it mean to be fair?
5. What is the difference between treating people fairly and treating people equally?

HOW TO PRESENT CHANGE TO EMPLOYEES

Competency: Leading Change

Description: This experiential activity introduces participants to a model for introducing change to employees, and also provides opportunities for the participants to apply the model to the change process.

Goals:

- Identify ways to involve employees in the change process.
- Create a structured process for introducing change to employees.
- Develop strategies for gaining employee commitment to the change.

Time Required: 1.5–2 hours

Preparation and Materials:

- *How to Present Change to Employees* (one per participant)
- Flip chart pages
- Markers
- Masking tape

Process:

1. Introduce the activity by mentioning that in today's organizations, change is the rule rather than the exception. Downsizing, reorganization, rapid growth, new technology, and a diverse workforce are creating more pressures and placing more demands on employees at all levels to manage and deal with the challenges of change.

2. Ask participants to give examples of specific changes their employees are experiencing, have experienced recently, or will experience in the near future. Capture their responses on flip chart pages. You may want to prompt them by identifying categories or types of changes, such as policies, procedures, technology, restructuring, or downsizing.

3. Explain that the manager is the key to change. As a change agent, the manager is expected to facilitate a specific change easily and effectively with a minimum of disruption and with maximum support from the group. *How* the manager introduces change is often the determining factor in the more successful transitions and transformations. Tell them that although there is no "easy way" to deal with change, you are going to introduce them to a process for presenting change to an individual or group.

4. Distribute a copy of *How to Present Change to Employees* to each participant. Ask them to read the handout and jot down any questions they may have as they read through the process. Give them about 5 minutes.

5. At the end of the 5 minutes, solicit questions from the group and clarify as needed.

6. Tell them that *planning* is an important part of the process, and that they should spend a significant amount of time thinking about what they are going to say, how they are going to say it, and how employees are going to react. People often resist change for two major reasons: (1) they don't understand the reasons for the change, and (2) they see no benefit to them personally. Managers who address these concerns up front are more likely to gain employee support for the change.

7. Form seven subgroups. Ask the subgroups to follow the process outlined in *How to Present Change to Employees*, instructing them to write down what they would say or do in preparation for presenting to their employees the organization's plan to implement a new computer system. Allow 20 minutes for the task.

8. At the end of the 20 minutes, assign each subgroup a specific section of the process, and ask for a volunteer from each subgroup to record the questions or action items for that particular section on flip chart pages and post them on the wall. Review each section, soliciting comments and questions from the group and modifying the flip chart pages as appropriate.

9. Discuss this part of the activity, asking the following questions:
   - What was your reaction to this planning process?
   - What was similar to or different from what you normally would do in presenting a change to your employees?
   - How is this process going to help you the next time you have to present a change to your employees?

10. Tell participants that because they now have a better understanding of how to plan to present change, you are going to give them the opportunity to apply what they learned. As a large group, identify three scenarios from the list of change examples created earlier. Explain that these three scenarios will be used for role playing.

11. Divide the group into trios. Explain that on a rotating basis, each member of the trio will have an opportunity to practice the role of (a) the manager, who will present the change to the employee; (b) the employee, who will react to the manager's message; and (c) an observer, who will give feedback to the manager.

(Continued)

12. Ask the participants to assign one of the three scenarios to each of their trio members and tell them they have 15 minutes to plan what they are going to say when presenting their change.

13. At the end of the 15 minutes, call time and explain that on a rotating basis, each member of each trio will present his or her change to the employee. Explain that each round should be 10 minutes of role playing, followed by 5 minutes of feedback from the observer. The observer should focus on identifying what the manager did well in following the process and what he or she could have done better.

14. Begin the first round, and call time after 10 minutes, giving them a 2-minute warning before calling time. Direct them to give feedback, calling time after 5 minutes and then announcing the second round. Repeat the process for the second and third rounds.

15. After participants have completed all three rounds, reconvene the entire group for a general discussion of the key learning points and the value of the activity.

Discussion:
1. How did it feel to present the change following the model?
2. What was your reaction as an employee receiving information about the change?
3. What did you learn from your observer's feedback?
4. What new insights did you gain about introducing change to employees?
5. What are you going to do differently when introducing change in the future?

Variations:
- To shorten the activity, eliminate the rotating trio role-play (steps 10 through 15), or conduct one round instead of three.
- If you have fewer than fourteen people, assign more than one section to each subgroup during step 8.

How to Present Change to Employees

The following outlines a process for presenting change to employees.

Prepare

- Gather as much background information as you can.
- Think about how different people will react to and be affected by the change.
- Empathize—try to put yourself in your employees' shoes.
- Plan how you are going to introduce the change—that is, exactly what you are going to say.
- Anticipate their questions and plan your responses.

Deliver Your Message

- Explain the change's purpose.
  - Give background information.
  - Explain the reason or reasons for the change as fully as you can.
  - Tie the change to the "big picture," explaining how it relates to solving an organizational or departmental problem or some other kind of improvement.
- Explain the change's impact.
  - Communicate honestly how the change will affect the people involved.
  - Be enthusiastic and positive, but deal openly and frankly with the negative aspects.
- Provide information.
  - Supply details about the change, including what they can expect and what is expected of them.
  - Stress the personal benefits and potential opportunities for them.
  - Assure them that they will receive training and support as appropriate to the situation.
- Handle concerns.
  - Solicit questions and concerns.
  - Listen and respond openly, taking whatever time is necessary to fully give them opportunities to express their feelings.
- Involve employees in the change.
  - Ask people for help and commitment in making the change work.
  - Actively seek their input and suggestions, and ask them about any problems they may have or anticipate.

(Continued)

- Use group problem solving to overcome problems and address related issues.
- Ask for their ideas on how to implement the change.

Follow Up

- Check in with people periodically to find out how they are handling the change.
- Continue to offer support and serve as a sounding board when needed.
- Recognize and reward those who support the change through their efforts, advice, and input.

Source: "Management Model for Change: Presenting Change to Employees" by Karen Lawson in *2008 Pfeiffer Annual: Consulting* (2008). Reproduced by permission of Pfeiffer, an Imprint of Wiley.

LEADING CHANGE

Competency: Leading Change

Description: This activity addresses the leader's role in leading change downward, across, and upward in order to become a more resilient leader, build a resilient workforce, and create a resilient organization.

Goals:

- Identify the behaviors that help lead change.
- Select strategies for influencing change at all levels.

Time Required: 30 minutes

Materials and Preparation:

- *Leading Change at Every Level* (one per participant)
- Flip chart pages
- Markers
- Masking tape

Process:

1. Introduce the activity by explaining that change is inevitable, and that effective leaders must become adept at dealing with, managing, and leading change.
2. Divide the group into subgroups of five or six and ask them to respond to the following questions and post their responses on flip chart pages. Give them 10 minutes.
   - What are the three major changes in your industry?
   - What are the three major changes in your organization?
   - What is the impact of these changes on you?
   - What is the impact of these changes on your employees?
3. After 10 minutes, reconvene the group and compare their responses to the questions.
4. Point out that before we can be successful change leaders, we need to start by taking a cold, hard look at our own behaviors and attitudes. Change starts with us "modeling the way" by what we say and do. According to James O'Toole, author of *Leading Change: Overcoming the Ideology of Comfort and the Tyranny of Custom* (1995), "To overcome the resistance to change, one must be willing, for starters, to change oneself."
5. Explain that after they have dealt with change themselves, effective leaders are able to lead change in all directions: upward, downward, and horizontally.

(Continued)

6. Distribute the *Leading Change at Every Level* model to participants. Briefly discuss the four levels.

7. As a group, choose one example of organizational change they identified earlier.

8. Divide the group into four subgroups and assign each group a different level: self, subordinates and team members, peers and other change leaders, and superiors.

9. Ask subgroup members to give specific examples of what they are doing, have done, or can do to lead change at the level they were assigned, keeping the change example in mind. Ask them to post their responses on flip chart pages. Give them 15 minutes.

10. At the end of the 15 minutes, reconvene the entire group and review the responses of each subgroup.

Discussion Questions:
1. What did you learn about the leader's role in leading change?
2. How adept have you been in leading change at every level?
3. On which level or levels do you need to focus?

Variation:
• Rather than asking participants to select a change they are experiencing, you may assign one of your choosing.

LEADING CHANGE AT EVERY LEVEL

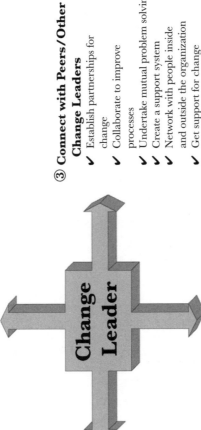

④ Communicate with Senior Management
- ❯ Be proactive—take risks
- ❯ Offer solutions
- ❯ Keep others informed
- ❯ Align goals and priorities

③ Connect with Peers/Other Change Leaders
- ❯ Establish partnerships for change
- ❯ Collaborate to improve processes
- ❯ Undertake mutual problem solving
- ❯ Create a support system
- ❯ Network with people inside and outside the organization
- ❯ Get support for change projects

① Challenge Yourself
- ❯ Reengineer yourself
- ❯ Seek opportunities
- ❯ Manage stress
- ❯ Assess yourself and your needs
- ❯ Recognize your own resistance
- ❯ Take risks
- ❯ Learn new skills and behaviors

② Involve Direct Reports/Team Members
- ❯ Set high expectations
- ❯ Give clear direction
- ❯ Provide reinforcement, reward, recognition
- ❯ Clarify roles
- ❯ Give frequent feedback
- ❯ Establish and celebrate quick wins
- ❯ Encourage risk taking
- ❯ Meet people where they are
- ❯ Make room for creativity

MAKE THEM LAUGH

Competency: Humor

Description: This activity gives participants an opportunity to find humor in everyday workplace situations and to explore how having a sense of humor can enhance a leader's effectiveness.

Goals:

- Explain the importance of having a sense of humor.
- Identify the benefits of humor in the work environment.
- Identify ways to add fun to the workplace.

Time Required: 40 minutes

Materials and Preparation:

- Variety of cartoons cut from newspapers or magazines without the captions
- *Benefits of Humor* (one per participant)
- *Ideas for Putting Fun in the Workplace* (one per participant)
- Flip chart pages
- Markers
- Masking tape

Process:

1. Introduce the activity by explaining that having a sense of humor is an important characteristic of an effective leader. A manager who demonstrates a good sense of humor creates an open and relaxed work environment in which people can flourish.

2. Divide the group into subgroups of four or five and ask them to develop a list of the benefits of laughter and humor in the workplace. Give them 5 minutes.

3. At the end of the 5 minutes, reconvene the entire group and solicit their ideas, posting these on flip chart pages.

4. Distribute *Benefits of Humor* and compare the list with the one the group generated. Ask participants for examples of how they have seen evidence of these benefits in their work environment.

5. Explain that anyone, even the most serious person, can develop a sense of humor. All it takes is a little practice. Tell them that you are going to give them an opportunity to find the humor in everyday work-related situations.

6. Divide the group again into subgroups. Distribute one or more of the cartoons to each of the subgroups. Also, assign each subgroup a different business-related topic or theme (such as change, customer service, sales, new products, new procedures, and so on) and ask them to write a humorous caption for the cartoon related to the theme. Give them 10 minutes.

7. Reconvene the group and ask representatives from the subgroups to present their cartoons and captions to the entire group.

8. Ask them to once again return to their subgroups and to make a list of things they as individual leaders can do to further develop a sense humor and to add humor to the workplace. Ask the subgroups to record their ideas on flip chart pages and post these on the walls. Give them 10 minutes.

9. After the lists have been posted, compare them. Also distribute *Ideas for Putting Fun in the Workplace,* and discuss how participants might implement some of the ideas.

Discussion:
1. What did you experience as you were working together to write the captions?
2. How can further developing your sense of humor help you as a leader?
3. Which ideas are you going to implement?

Variations:
- You can use photos instead of or in addition to the cartoons.
- You may choose to give the same cartoons or pictures to each group.
- You may give the same theme to each group.
- You could give examples of jokes for which participants provide the punch lines.

BENEFITS OF HUMOR

The following are the benefits of using humor to create an environment in which employees can flourish.

- Boosts morale
- Reduces stress
- Increases energy
- Reduces tension
- Increases productivity
- Strengthens bonds among coworkers
- Creates rapport with customers
- Persuades others to see your point of view
- Builds trust
- Stimulates creative thinking and problem solving
- Reduces complaints
- Encourages communication
- Increases workplace satisfaction
- Improves self-esteem
- Engages employees

IDEAS FOR PUTTING FUN IN THE WORKPLACE

The following are some quick, easy, and low-cost or no-cost ways you can put fun in your workplace.

• Hang humorous posters, ads, pictures, and cartoons.

• Add a humorous quotation or picture to your e-mail signature.

• Place a few toys on your desk and bookcase.

• Hold up an "applause" sign or use a "hand clapper" to congratulate someone for doing something like completing a project, exceeding sales numbers, or overcoming a major obstacle.

• Establish a "Fun Committee" that is responsible for coming up with fresh ideas for infusing fun into the workplace.

• Create a humor bulletin board and encourage people to post funny (and nonoffensive) cartoons and jokes. Assign someone to monitor it for appropriateness.

• Have fun dress-up days for celebrations, such as Halloween, St. Patrick's Day, or April Fools' Day. You could also have an ugly tie or scarf day, or something similar.

• Add relevant cartoons or funny quotations to meeting notices and agendas.

SHOWING APPRECIATION

Competency: Motivating

Description: This small-group activity gives participants an opportunity to share with each other ideas and techniques they may be using to reward and recognize employees. This activity also prompts them to generate and implement new ideas to show their employees how much they appreciate them.

Goals:

- Identify ways to reward and recognize employees.
- Explain how showing appreciation helps create a positive motivational climate.

Time Required: 30 minutes

Materials and Preparation:

- Flip chart pages
- Markers
- Masking tape

Process:

1. Introduce the activity by explaining that an effective leader knows how to create an environment that encourages and promotes employee self-motivation. Point out that one technique for creating that environment is to use appropriate methods of reward and reinforcement.

2. Explain that to be effective, rewards must be (1) tied to specific performance and (2) valued by the employee. Tell them to keep these two points in mind as they participate in this activity.

3. Divide the group into subgroups of five to seven and give each subgroup two flip chart pages and markers.

4. Ask them to write "Organization" on one flip chart page and "Individual Managers" on another. Then ask them to discuss and then list on the flip chart pages specific ways the organization and individual managers can recognize and reward employees. Tell them to focus on nontraditional means of showing appreciation and recognizing "beyond-the-call-of-duty" performance. Give them 15 minutes.

5. At the end of the 15 minutes, ask the subgroups to post their lists on the wall.

6. Ask the participants to compare the lists, pointing out similar ideas and focusing on ideas that may be new and innovative. Ask participants to share specific examples of how some of these techniques had an impact on the employees.

Discussion:
1. What are some ideas or techniques you see listed that you had not thought of before?
2. How do these various ideas or techniques relate to our criteria of being (1) tied to specific performance and (2) valued by the employee?
3. How do these techniques create a positive motivational climate?
4. Which of these ideas are you going to implement?

Variations:
- If time is limited, ask some subgroups to address ideas for the "organization" and others to address ideas for "individual managers."
- In a multisession program, ask participants to identify one idea or technique to implement prior to the next session and be ready to share the results with the rest of the group during the next session.

TELL ME A STORY

Competency: Storytelling

Description: In this activity, participants will learn how to use stories to convey corporate values and priorities, share lessons learned, or highlight desired behaviors.

Goals:

- Recognize the benefit of using stories.
- Follow a structured approach to developing a story.
- Identify situations in which participants can use stories to convey their message.

Time Required: 45–60 minutes

Materials and Preparation:

- A story of your own (or someone else's) that follows the model presented in the *Developing Your Story Worksheet*
- *Developing Your Story Worksheet* (one per participant)

Process:

1. Introduce the activity by explaining that stories have been used to captivate audiences throughout the ages. Stories teach a lesson as well as entertain. Throughout history, stories have been passed from generation to generation as a means of preserving a group's culture, heritage, history, and traditions. Stories are at the very heart of who we are as human beings. They reach in and grab at the core of our existence. They help us define who we are and what we believe, and for that very reason corporate leaders use personal stories to enhance their presentations, make a point, and teach a lesson.

2. Ask participants for examples of stories they have heard that made an impression on them. Discuss why the stories were memorable.

3. Explain that they are going to learn how to construct stories that will make their points more memorable.

4. Distribute the *Developing Your Story Worksheet* and review the elements. Ask them to follow the worksheet and take notes as you tell your story.

5. After you have told your story, ask people to work in pairs or small groups to compare their notes, identifying specific things you said in your story that illustrated each step in the storytelling process. Give them 5 minutes.

6. At the end of the 5 minutes, reconvene the entire group and solicit examples for each step in the storytelling model.

7. Next explain that they will have an opportunity to develop their own stories.

8. Put people into subgroups of three or four. Ask them to identify one person in their subgroup who is willing to share or develop a story that illustrates a key point they would like to make or message they would like to convey. Possible categories include the following: corporate values, customer service, doing the right thing, or making a tough decision.

9. Give participants 20 minutes to work in their subgroups outlining a story they will be sharing with the entire group.

10. At the end of the 20 minutes, reconvene the entire group and ask a representative from each subgroup to share his or her subgroup's story. After each story, solicit reactions from the group.

11. After all stories have been told, conduct a general discussion.

Discussion:

1. What did you experience as you were developing your story?

2. What was your reaction to listening to the stories?

3. What stories can you tell to convey your message?

4. How can you use this technique of storytelling to increase your effectiveness as a leader?

Variations:

- Rather than providing categories in step 8, solicit categories from the group.
- Provide a written transcript of a story and have people work in groups to dissect it according to the model presented in the worksheet.

Developing Your Story Worksheet

Topic: **Story Title:**

- *Determine the story's purpose.*
  - Express the key learning point or message you want to convey.
  - Clarify what you want the audience to do (or think about) differently.
- *Create the context.*
  - Describe the setting and situation.
  - Introduce the characters (and give them names).
  - Begin the story and journey (and convey action).
- *Introduce the challenge or complication.*
  - Describe the complication, problem, obstacle, or conflict.
  - Relate the situation to the audience's experience.
- *Share the resolution.*
  - Reveal the turning point of the story, or how the character overcomes the obstacle.
  - Show how the character experiences a recognition, disclosure, or discovery.
- *Bring it to a conclusion.*
  - Communicate what you want the audience to take from the experience.
  - Make your point (or lesson learned).

What Do Your Employees Value?

Competency: Motivating

Description: In this activity, participants explore the concept of creating a positive motivational climate for each employee by speculating on what each employee values.

Goals:

- Develop a process for discovering what each employee values.
- Identify specific ways to motivate each employee.

Time Required: 45 minutes

Materials and Preparation:

- *What's Important to You?* (one per participant)
- *What My Employees Value* (one per participant)

Process:

1. Introduce the activity by stating, "Managers often ask, 'How do I find out what motivates my employees?' The best way is to talk to your employees and really listen to them. They will let you know indirectly, and sometimes even directly, what's important to them."
2. Tell them that another way of discovering what is important to employees is to ask them directly by having them complete a survey in which they rank the top five items of greatest importance to them.
3. Distribute the *What's Important to You?* survey and ask participants to complete it for themselves, identifying the top five items of greatest importance to them and ranking them from 1 (most important) to 5 (least important). Ask them to set aside the completed surveys.
4. Distribute the *What My Employees Value* matrix. Ask them to write the names of their employees across the top. Then ask them to place a check mark next to the items they think each of their employees will check.

Discussion:

1. How do the checked items on your own survey compare to the items you believe your employees would check? How similar or different are the lists?
2. What is the reason you think your personal list is similar to or different from those of your employees?

(Continued)

3. What do you think your employees' reactions would be if you were to ask them to complete the survey?

4. How could you use this information to create a more positive motivational climate for each person in your work unit?

Variations:

• Suggest that participants ask each of their employees to complete the survey and return it to them. Once they receive the surveys, the managers should each compare their checked list with those of their employees to see how well they really know their group.

• You may suggest that each participant create his or her own survey by deleting some elements on this survey and adding others of his or her choosing.

• In a multisession program, give this as an assignment between sessions.

WHAT'S IMPORTANT TO YOU?

Please identify the top five items of greatest importance to you and rank them from 1 (most important) to 5 (least important).

_____ Additional responsibility

_____ Public praise and recognition

_____ Private praise and recognition

_____ Personal time off (ability to leave early, and so on)

_____ Flexible hours

_____ Leading a team

_____ Chance for promotion

_____ Variety of assignments

_____ Education/training opportunities

_____ Cash bonus

_____ Tangible, nonmonetary rewards

_____ More decision-making opportunities

_____ Helping to set goals

WHAT MY EMPLOYEES VALUE

Write down the names of your employees across the top of this matrix. Next, place a check mark next to the items you think each employee will check.

Employees' Name:	What They Value						
Additional responsibility							
Public praise and recognition							
Private praise and recognition							
Personal time off (ability to leave early, and so on)							
Flexible hours							
Leading a team							
Chance for promotion							
Variety of assignments							
Education/training opportunities							
Cash bonus							
Tangible, nonmonetary rewards							
More decision-making opportunities							
Helping to set goals							

CHAPTER SEVEN

DEVELOPING AND MANAGING

S uccessful leaders are effective in developing people and managing their performance. Some of the activities in this chapter address critical competencies for developing employees, such as delegating, coaching, and mentoring. Other activities are designed to help leaders set clear expectations for their employees, provide appropriate feedback, and identify ways to hold them accountable.

APPLYING YOUR COACHING SKILLS

Competency: Coaching

Description: This activity introduces participants to a structured performance improvement coaching session with an employee.

Goals:
- Identify the steps used to plan for a performance improvement coaching session.
- Apply a coaching plan to participants' own work situations.

Time Required: 60–90 minutes

Materials and Preparation:
- *Applying Your Coaching Skills* (one per participant)

Process:
1. Introduce the activity by noting that in today's organizations, coaching is an integral part of the overall performance management system. Further explain that coaching is an ongoing process of providing employees with the frequent and consistent feedback—positive and negative—they need to succeed in today's fast-paced and constantly changing workplace.
2. Mention that there are two types of structured coaching:
   - Performance improvement coaching is appropriate when the employee is not meeting standards or expectations.
   - Developmental coaching is used when the employee is meeting expectations, but you want to help him or her reach the next level of success.
3. Emphasize that for the purpose of this activity, participants will be focusing on performance improvement coaching.
4. Also mention that they should spend a significant amount of time planning for a performance improvement coaching session.
5. Tell them they will have an opportunity to practice planning for a performance improvement coaching session with an employee. Distribute a copy of *Applying Your Coaching Skills* to each participant.
6. Create subgroups of four or five. Ask subgroup members to identify a coaching subject from one of them, and then to work through the worksheet together. Tell them they should appoint a spokesperson who will be responsible for presenting their coaching plan to the entire group. Give them 20 minutes.

7. At the end of the 20 minutes, reconvene the entire group and ask the spokesperson for each subgroup to present the subgroup's plan.
8. After the last presentation, conduct a general discussion.

Discussion:
1. What is your reaction to the coaching planning sheet?
2. How is this similar to or different from the approach you use to coach employees?
3. How can you use this to plan for the coaching sessions with your employees?

Variations:
- Rather than creating subgroups, you can ask each person to map out an individual coaching plan.
- In a multisession program, you can use this as an individual assignment between sessions.
- Once the subgroups have outlined their coaching plan, you could have them role-play within their subgroups.
- You can assign one coaching scenario for all subgroups to work through.

APPLYING YOUR COACHING SKILLS

Identify an employee whose performance is not meeting your standards and expectations. Then map out a plan for your coaching session with this employee.

- Name of employee:

- Job or task:

- What are your standards or expectations for this job or task?

- How does the employee's actual performance differ from the desired performance? Be specific.

- What data or evidence do you have to show that the performance is below expectations?

- What factors might be affecting the employee's performance? What obstacles or barriers might be preventing the employee from meeting your expectations?

- What are the consequences or potential outcomes if the employee does not improve performance?

- Where and when are you going to hold the coaching session?

- What are you going to say at the beginning of the coaching session?

- What open-ended questions might you ask to diagnose the problem, to unearth any underlying issues, or to identify extenuating circumstances that may be causing the performance problem?

- What open-ended questions could you ask to get the employee to identify what he or she needs to do to improve performance?

- What open-ended questions could you ask to gain the employee's commitment to improving his or her performance?

- How will you monitor the employee's performance?

- What will you do to support the employee's efforts to improve performance?

CREATING A TEAM IDENTITY

Competency: Team Building

Description: This activity is designed to help participants recognize the importance and benefits of developing a sense of cohesiveness among team members.

Goal:

- Explore ways to create a sense of identity among team members.

Time Required: 60 minutes

Materials and Preparation:

- Flip chart pages
- Markers
- Masking tape

Process:

1. Begin the activity by asking people to work in pairs to develop a definition of a team. Give them three minutes, and then solicit responses from the group. (Many people offer this definition: "A group of people working toward a common goal.") Point out that this is only part of the definition. People working in the same department may have a common goal, but they may not see themselves as part of a team.

2. Post the following definition on a flip chart page: "A team is a group of highly interdependent people working toward a common goal. They experience personal satisfaction by identifying with each other and with the team as a whole. They rely on group collaboration to solve problems and achieve team success." Discuss their reaction to the definition.

3. Explain that effective team leaders help to create a sense of identity and cohesiveness among team members.

4. Divide the group into subgroups of five to seven. Explain that the purpose of the activity is to create a slogan for each of the teams they have just formed. The slogan is to represent the team's values, its purpose, and anything else that distinguishes the team. Suggest that they begin the activity with a discussion of their team's values, purpose, and so on. The finished product is to be presented on a sheet of flip chart paper. Give them 30 minutes.

5. At the end of the 30 minutes, ask each team to post its slogan on the wall.

6. Ask members of each team to present their slogan to the rest of the group and explain the rationale for the design.

(Continued)

Discussion:

1. What was your reaction to creating a team slogan?
2. How did you go about doing it?
3. What did you learn from the activity?
4. How can you use this activity to help your team be more effective?

Variations:

- For a group of people from the same organization, you may ask participants to create a slogan that represents the entire organization.
- You may want to create the subgroup teams by using some criteria, such as similar job functions, personality styles, and so on.
- Instead of coming up with a slogans, participants could create logos or identify songs, movies titles, television shows, or book titles that reflect each team's purpose and values.

DELEGATION CASE STUDY

Competency: Delegating

Description: This case study activity gives participants an opportunity to explore the appropriate behavior a leader should use when delegating an assignment to an employee.

Goals:

• Identify effective delegation behaviors.

• Recognize the impact on an employee when delegation is not done properly.

Time Required: 40–45 minutes

Materials and Preparation:

• *Case Study: How to Delegate Effectively* (one per participant)

Process:

1. Introduce the activity by explaining that managers frequently complain that they have too much to do and too little time in which to do it. Unchecked, this feeling leads to stress and managerial ineffectiveness. In many cases, managers could greatly reduce their stress by practicing a critical management skill—delegation. Point out that if delegation is not done properly, it can have a negative impact on the employee.

2. Distribute copies of *Case Study: How to Delegate Effectively* and ask participants to read it individually. Give them 5 to 7 minutes.

3. At the end of the time period, form subgroups of four to six people and ask them to discuss the case, particularly focusing on what the manager did well and what he or she could do better. Give them 15 minutes.

4. At the end of the 15 minutes, reconvene the group for a general discussion.

Discussion:

1. What did the manager do well in delegating to the employee?

2. What could he or she have done better?

3. What was the employee's reaction?

4. How well do you think the employee would do in fulfilling the assignment as the manager presented it?

(Continued)

5. What specifically would you do differently as a delegator?

6. How is your own behavior different from or similar to the manager's behavior in the case study?

7. What did you learn from this activity?

8. How can this help you the next time you delegate an assignment?

Variation:

• Instead of using this as a small-group case study activity, you could conduct this as a scripted role-play by asking for two volunteers to read the roles of Terry and Pat in front of the entire group. You would ask the group to give examples of what Terry did well and what he or she could have done better.

CASE STUDY: HOW TO DELEGATE EFFECTIVELY

Read the following case study and discuss what the manager did well and what he or she could do better:

Manager (Terry): Pat, I'd like to talk to you about taking on a new assignment. As you know, it's very important that the new employees be trained properly and brought up to speed as quickly as possible. Do you agree?

Employee (Pat): Absolutely. We really need help around here right away.

Terry: Well, I think it's important to begin to develop the experienced employees by giving them an opportunity to learn new skills and expand their responsibilities. So I have identified you as one of the potential employees who would assume the responsibility of training all the new hires. I have chosen you because not only do you do your job well but also you have the qualities that are important in a good trainer. You are well organized, patient, empathetic, and creative, and you express yourself well. I believe you would be a good role model for new employees. Are you interested?

Pat: I guess so.

Terry: Let me tell you a little more about what I expect and what the assignment involves. First of all, you would have complete freedom to design how you want to conduct the training and to decide what should be included. I would like you to develop a written plan that we can use on an ongoing basis. I would also suggest that you take advantage of the experience and expertise of some of your coworkers. They may have some good ideas to contribute. I know I'm hitting you with this cold, but off the top of your head, do you have any thoughts or ideas on how you think the training should be handled?

Pat: I'm not really sure. I guess I would need some time to think about it, but I do know that the way I was taught is not the way it should be done. Basically, I learned on my own by trial and error.

Terry: Well, you can certainly draw on that experience as an example of what not to do. Do you have any concerns or misgivings about the assignment?

Pat: I really don't know anything about how to train—that is, on a formal basis. And then, what about my other responsibilities? This is going to take a lot of time.

Terry: I'm glad you brought that up. First of all, you and I will need to work out a plan and identify what duties of yours we can assign to some others without burdening any one person, as well as those tasks you feel you need to continue to do yourself. As far as your other concern, maybe we can find some train-the-trainer program to send you to. You

(Continued)

could call the state trade association and ask if they know whom you might contact about such a program. Do you feel a little more comfortable now?

Pat: I guess so.

Terry: Does it sound like something you would like to do?

Pat: Sure, I'll give it a try.

Terry: Great. I know you'll do a good job. What I'd like to do is to meet with you at the end of every week just to get an idea of where you are and identify if there's anything you need in terms of additional resources. But keep in mind that this is your project. I'm here to give you support and serve as a sounding board, but I want you to develop this yourself. How does that sound?

Pat: Good. I think I can handle it.

Terry: I have no doubt. So let's plan on getting together next Friday to take a look at your preliminary plan.

DELEGATING EFFECTIVELY SELF-ASSESSMENT

Competency: Delegating

Description: This self-assessment activity is designed to help participants identify their effectiveness in delegating assignments to others.

Goals:

- Heighten awareness of participants' delegation strengths and weaknesses.
- Develop an action plan to become a more effective delegator.

Time Required: 30–40 minutes

Materials and Preparation:

- *Delegating Effectively Self-Assessment* (one per participant)

Process:

1. Introduce the activity by explaining that delegation is a critical management skill, and that the failure to delegate effectively has led to the downfall of many leaders.
2. Explain that participants will have an opportunity to gain insight into their delegation skills by responding to a self-assessment.
3. Distribute the *Delegating Effectively Self-Assessment* and tell them they have 10 minutes to complete it and score it.
4. Reconvene the group and explain that the purpose of a self-assessment is to increase their awareness and understanding of the behaviors that may be keeping them from being as effective as they would like to be.
5. Ask them to review their overall total as well as specific items to which they responded "seldom" or "almost never." Ask for volunteers to share those items they would like to improve.

Discussion:

1. What is your reaction to your self-assessment?
2. How did you feel about completing it?
3. What did you learn about your approach to delegating?
4. What insights did you gain?
5. How can these insights be helpful to you?

Variation:

- You can use this self-assessment with an individual in a coaching session.

DELEGATING EFFECTIVELY SELF-ASSESSMENT

Using the following key, indicate to what degree each of the following statements is characteristic of your actions or behavior.

	Almost Always (over 80%)	Often (61%–80%)	Sometimes (41%–60%)	Seldom (20%–40%)	Almost Never (less than 20%)
1. I delegate assignments to others on a regular basis.					
2. I make sure I "spread assignments around" rather than choosing the person I can always depend on.					
3. I take time to plan how I am going to present the assignment to the employee.					
4. I make sure the employee has adequate training to handle the assignment.					
5. I explain to the employee my reason for choosing him or her for the assignment by pointing out his or her specific skills, experience, or abilities that match the assignment's requirements.					
6. I give specific performance standards for the assignment, such as specific deadlines and appropriate parameters.					
7. I refrain from prescribing exactly how an assignment should be completed.					
8. I clearly explain what the assignment entails in terms of responsibility and accountability.					
9. I give the employee the appropriate authority or power to take action and make decisions related to the assignment.					

	Almost Always (over 80%)	Often (61%–80%)	Sometimes (41%–60%)	Seldom (20%–40%)	Almost Never (less than 20%)
10. I ask the employee to share any concerns he or she may have about taking on this assignment.					
11. I make sure the employee understands clearly what I am asking him or her to do by asking an open-ended question, such as "What is your understanding of what this assignment entails?" or something similar.					
12. I establish appropriate controls and check-points to monitor the progress of a delegated assignment.					
13. I express to the employee that I have complete confidence in his or her ability to handle this assignment successfully.					
14. I check in with the employee at various points as planned, just to make sure he or she is on track.					
15. I recognize and reward the employee for his or her successful completion of the assignment.					

Scoring: To find your overall delegating proficiency, simply count the number of check marks for each of the five columns. Give yourself a score for each check mark based on the following scale:

Column	Number of Checks	×	Rating Value	=	Total
Almost always		×	5	=	
Often		×	4	=	
Sometimes		×	3	=	
Seldom		×	2	=	
Almost never		×	1	=	
				Total Score:	

(Continued)

Compute the sums for each column by multiplying the number of check marks by the value for each rating. Once you have the number for each of the separate columns, add all of the numbers together to get your total score. This score reflects the habits you have demonstrated in the past. The insights gained from this assessment will help you identify your delegating strengths and improvement opportunities. Please refer to the categories and their point values to interpret your score:

70–75	**Effective delegator** Your staff members are lucky to have you as their leader.
55–69	**Inconsistent delegator** You tend to overlook some key elements of the delegation process.
40–54	**Developing delegator** Your tendency is to simply assign tasks rather than truly delegate an assignment.
20–39	**Struggling delegator** Your lack of delegation is preventing you from getting your own job done.
15–19	**Ineffective delegator** You probably feel stressed and overwhelmed. "Get help quickly!"

DELEGATION PROCESS

Competency: Delegating

Description: This activity introduces the participants to a structured process for delegating an assignment to an employee.

Goals:

- Explain the difference between delegation and task assignment.
- Identify a structured process for delegating an assignment to an employee.
- Apply the delegation to participants' own situations.

Time Required: 60 minutes

Materials and Preparation:

- *The Delegation Process* (one per participant)
- *Delegation Process Worksheet* (one per participant)
- Markers
- Flip chart pages

Process:

1. Introduce the activity by explaining that effective leaders have mastered a very critical skill—delegation.

2. Ask the participants to indicate by a show of hands if they think they are good delegators. (Few people will raise their hand.) Then ask those who did not raise their hand the reason they are not good delegators. Capture the responses on a flip chart. Typical responses are as follows:

   - "It takes too long to explain."
   - "No one on my staff is capable of doing it."
   - "If you want it done right, you have to do it yourself."
   - "My people are already overworked. I can't dump anything more on them."

3. Explain that these "reasons" are really excuses. The following are some of the "real reasons" managers don't delegate:

   - They are insecure—afraid the other person might do it better.
   - They want to do what they know how to do (or like to do), rather than spending time doing what they should be doing.
   - They have a low opinion of those to whom jobs should be delegated.
   - They don't want to take time to develop employees.

(Continued)

- They have poor organization skills.
- They fear being disliked.
- They have poor communication skills.
- They are perfectionists.
- They think, "If the other person 'messes up,' I'm still accountable."

4. Tell them that one major reason many managers are not good delegators is that they may not completely understand what delegation is. Explain that delegation is not task assignment. Task assignment is simply assigning work to an individual within the duties and responsibilities of his or her position. Delegation, however, involves the manager giving someone the responsibility and authority to do something that is normally part of the manager's job.

5. Explain that once they understand the difference between task assignment and delegation, the next step is to identify the delegation process.

6. Distribute a copy of *The Delegation Process* to each participant and conduct a brief lecture explaining the process of delegation.

   - Determine what you are going to delegate. Plan how you are going to present the assignment, including your requirements and parameters, the employee's authority level, checkpoints, and your expectations.

   - Choose the right person. Assess the skills and the experience of your employees as objectively as possible. Don't be too quick to choose the person whom you always know you can depend on.

   - Give an overview of the assignment, including the importance of the assignment and why you have chosen the employee for the job.

   - Describe the new responsibility in detail, outlining subtasks, defining any necessary parameters, and setting performance standards. Make sure the employee understands his or her level or degree of authority. Let the employee know whom he or she can turn to for help as well as other available resources.

   - Solicit questions, reactions, and suggestions. Ask the employee what approach he or she might take.

   - Listen to the employee's comments and respond empathetically. If the employee seems tentative, probe to uncover his or her concerns.

   - Ask the employee for commitment and offer help or some type of backup assistance. An employee who already feels overwhelmed may worry about completing existing assignments. It is your responsibility to help establish priorities and relieve some of the pressure by getting someone else to share some of the employee's routine tasks for the duration of the assignment.

- Be encouraging. Express confidence in the employee's ability to successfully handle the new responsibility.
- Establish checkpoints, deadlines, and ways to monitor progress. The entire discussion should be a collaborative process. You should strive for mutual agreement.
- Keep in contact and observe the checkpoints the two of you agreed to; however, don't hover. Remember, delegating means letting go.
- Recognize and reward the employee for his or her successful completion of the assignment.

7. Solicit from the group examples of assignments they could delegate but for which they currently are not doing so. Some possible examples are
   - Scheduling work hours, breaks, and so on
   - Reports
   - Proposals
   - Special projects
   - Research

8. Tell the participants they will now have an opportunity to practice delegating an assignment. Divide the group into subgroups of four or five, and ask members of each subgroup to identify an assignment they would like to delegate as well as a fictitious employee to whom they will delegate.

9. Distribute the *Delegation Process Worksheet* and ask subgroup members to write down what they would do or say in each step of the process in preparation for presenting the delegation assignment they identified in their subgroup. Tell them they have 20 minutes.

10. At the end of the 20 minutes, reconvene the group and ask a spokesperson from each subgroup to present a 5-minute summary of his or her subgroup's delegation process.

Discussion:

1. How was this process similar to or different from your own personal approach to delegating?
2. What is the benefit of this approach?
3. How do you think your employees would respond to this approach?
4. What are some assignments you are going to delegate?
5. What are you going to do differently?

(*Continued*)

Variations:

- Instead of having subgroup members choose their own delegation assignment, you can assign each group a different delegation topic or have all subgroups work on the same one (such as scheduling).
- You can use this as an individual assignment in a coaching situation.

THE DELEGATION PROCESS

The following is a step-by-step process for delegating an assignment.

1. Determine what you are going to delegate.

2. Choose the right person.

3. Give an overview of the assignment.

4. Describe the new responsibility in detail.

5. Solicit questions, reactions, and suggestions.

6. Listen to the employee's comments and respond empathetically.

7. Ask the employee for commitment and offer help.

8. Be encouraging.

9. Establish checkpoints, deadlines, and ways to monitor progress.

10. Keep in contact.

11. Recognize and reward the employee.

DELEGATION PROCESS WORKSHEET

For the delegation assignment your subgroup identified, write down what you would do or say for each step of the delegation process.

1. Determine what you are going to delegate.
   - Brief description of assignment
   - Parameters
   - Employee's authority level
   - Checkpoints
   - Expectations

2. Choose the right person (list the names of all employees you could consider).
   - Name   Skills   Experience
   - Person you selected:

3. Give an overview of the assignment.
   - Importance
   - Reasons you chose this person (refer to item 2)

4. Describe the new responsibility in detail.
   - Subtasks
   - Parameters
   - Deadlines
   - Performance standards
   - Employee's level of authority
   - Available resources (people)

5. Solicit questions, reactions, and suggestions.
   - Questions to check for understanding ("What is your understanding of what I'm asking you to do?")

- Questions to check for concerns ("What concerns or misgivings do you have?")

6. Listen to the employee's comments and respond empathetically.

7. Ask the employee for commitment and offer help.
    - Ways to relieve the employee's burden

    - Employee's priorities

8. Be encouraging.
    - Expression of confidence in the employee's ability

9. Establish checkpoints, deadlines, and ways to monitor progress.
    - Next meeting

    - Frequency of meetings

10. Keep in contact.
    - Checkpoints to be observed

11. Recognize and reward the employee.
    - Ways to recognize or reward the employee

DESCRIBING BEHAVIOR

Competencies: Coaching, Communicating, Giving Feedback, Managing Performance

Description: This activity is designed to help participants use specific, behavior-based statements when giving feedback or coaching an employee.

Goals:

- Be able to describe specific, observable behaviors demonstrated by an employee.
- Identify the difference between behavior-based and evaluative feedback.

Time Required: 20–30 minutes

Materials and Preparation:

- *Describing Behavior Worksheet* (one per participant)

Process:

1. Introduce the activity by explaining that the most difficult part of giving feedback (both positive and negative) to someone is being able to describe the person's behaviors in objective terms and not be judgmental. It is important to focus on behaviors that can be observed, measured, or discussed objectively. Feedback should also be stated in the context of specific incidents or situations.
2. Distribute the *Describing Behavior Worksheet* and ask the participants to work in pairs to complete it. Allow approximately 15 minutes.
3. After the participants have completed the worksheet, reconvene the group and ask for volunteers to share their responses. Solicit reactions from the rest of the group and offer suggestions as appropriate.

Discussion:

1. What was the most challenging or difficult aspect of the assignment?
2. If you were the recipient of this feedback, how would you react?
3. What is the most important thing you learned from doing this activity?
4. How can you apply what you learned to your own work environment?

Variation:

- If time is limited, assign each pair only one or two items from the *Describing Behavior Worksheet*.

DESCRIBING BEHAVIOR WORKSHEET

Turn each of the following evaluative statements or judgments into behavioral statements. Feel free to make up details and situations to create a context. When you create the feedback statement, phrase it as though you are addressing the person directly.

Example: Tom is not interested in this project.

Tom, you have missed every project deadline, and you come late to meetings.

1. Jason is arrogant.

2. Rosemary just doesn't "get it."

3. Duane is argumentative.

4. Ron is uncooperative.

5. Shondra is resistant to change.

6. Wendy has poor interpersonal skills.

7. Jack is lazy.

8. Darla is a team player.

9. Joachim shows good judgment.

10. Hank is very professional.

PERFORMANCE MANAGEMENT SKILLS CHECKLIST

Competency: Managing Performance

Description: This checklist activity presents a step-by-step approach to conducting a performance appraisal interview and gives participants an opportunity to identify the key behaviors they currently use as well as those they need to improve.

Goals:

• Identify steps in the performance appraisal interview.

• Assess participants' skills in conducting a performance appraisal interview.

Time Required: 30 minutes

Materials and Preparation:

• Flip chart page or slide on which the following questions are displayed:
   • What items do you need to work on?
   • What is getting in the way of your becoming a super performance manager?
   • What can you do to overcome these obstacles?

• *Performance Management Skills Checklist* (one per participant)

Process:

1. Introduce the activity by explaining to the participants that they will have an opportunity to take a look at how they currently conduct a performance appraisal interview.

2. Distribute the *Performance Management Skills Checklist* and tell them they have 10 minutes to complete the self-assessment.

3. At the end of the time period, form subgroups of four or five people. Display the following questions and ask participants to spend 10 minutes discussing them in their subgroups:
   • What items do you need to work on?
   • What is getting in the way of your becoming a super performance manager?
   • What can you do to overcome these obstacles?

4. Reconvene the group for a general discussion.

Discussion:

1. What was your reaction to your self-assessment?

2. What did you learn about the performance management process?

3. What did you learn about your approach to the performance management process?

4. What is getting in the way of your becoming a super performance manager?

5. How can the insights you gained from this self-assessment help you in managing your employees' performance?

Variations:

• You can use this as an individual activity in a one-on-one coaching situation.

• This assessment can be used as an assignment to be completed prior the classroom session or as an assignment in a multisession leadership development program.

PERFORMANCE MANAGEMENT SKILLS CHECKLIST

Think about your approach to performance management and especially the performance appraisal interview. As you read each of the following items, think about what you actually do before, during, and after the session, and answer accordingly by placing a check mark in either the "yes" or the "no" column.

Do you . . .

	Yes	No
1. Set performance standards and expectations and communicate them well in advance of the period to which they apply?	☐	☐
2. Provide day-to-day feedback on performance?	☐	☐
3. Conduct regular progress reviews with your employees?	☐	☐
4. Record objective facts concerning actual performance as they occur?	☐	☐
5. Record only job-related behavior?	☐	☐
6. Record direct observations rather than relying on "hearsay" from others?	☐	☐
7. Record both positive and negative behaviors rather than emphasizing either kind?	☐	☐
8. Keep the same basic format and level of detail of documentation for each employee?	☐	☐
9. Maintain documentation on all employees in a given work group?	☐	☐
10. Periodically review the collective documentation to be sure that the desired quantity, quality, and consistency of work are being maintained?	☐	☐
11. Avoid focusing on just the most recent and most easily remembered events?	☐	☐
12. Make sure that all issues are discussed when they occur so that there are no surprises during the performance appraisal interview?	☐	☐
13. Ask the employee to prepare for the performance appraisal interview?	☐	☐
14. Schedule the performance appraisal interview at a time that is mutually agreeable to both you and the employee?	☐	☐
15. Choose the appropriate location to eliminate distractions?	☐	☐
16. Avoid sitting with a physical barrier (such as a desk or table) between you and the employee during a performance appraisal interview?	☐	☐
17. Describe specific behavior that can be observed or measured— that is, specifically what the person did or said in the context of specific incidents or situations?	☐	☐

18. Avoid using evaluative or judgmental words, such as "good," ☐ ☐
    "bad," "poor," or "excellent?"
19. Use open-ended questions to help the employee explore his or ☐ ☐
    her own performance during the past evaluation period?
20. Use active listening techniques, such as paraphrasing, throughout the ☐ ☐
    performance appraisal interview to ensure clarity and understanding?
21. Periodically summarize key points covered during the discussion? ☐ ☐
22. Explain your perceptions of the employee's accomplishments ☐ ☐
    and areas for improvement, including your rationale for the rating?
23. Make sure that the discussion is close to a 50-50 exchange? ☐ ☐
24. State clearly what you want the person to do differently? ☐ ☐
25. Point out the positive consequences or benefits of the person ☐ ☐
    changing his or her behavior as you have described?
26. Ask the individual his or her understanding of the situation? ☐ ☐
27. Ask the individual what he or she is going to do to change ☐ ☐
    behavior or improve performance?
28. Work with the employee to devise a performance improvement plan? ☐ ☐
29. Devise an action plan with the employee that includes specific ☐ ☐
    dates and accountabilities?
30. Schedule and conduct follow-up sessions? ☐ ☐

Scoring: To get a clear picture of your performance management skills and practices, count the number of "yes" responses. Then read the following categories to identify your level of performance management proficiency.

26–30	**Super performance manager**
	You are doing an excellent job working with your employees to manage their performance. Keep up the good work.
21–25	**Credible performance manager**
	You are doing an effective job; however, there is some room for improvement.
16–20	**Hit-or-miss performance manager**
	Your performance management practices are sporadic. You often miss valuable opportunities to manage and improve your employees' performance.
0–15	**Rookie performance manager**
	You have a lot to learn.

STOPPING THE BLAME GAME

Competency: Accountability, Questioning

Description: This activity is designed to help participants learn how to hold people accountable for their actions by asking them the right open-ended questions.

Goals:

- Use open-ended questions to hold others accountable for their actions.
- Adopt an accountability mind-set and language.

Time Required: 30–40 minutes

Materials and Preparation:

- *Stopping the Blame Game Worksheet* (one per participant)

Process:

1. Introduce the activity by explaining that effective leaders create a culture of individual and organizational accountability by first taking ownership of their own decisions, policies, and actions. They also hold others accountable for their actions by stopping people from assigning blame or making excuses.

2. Ask participants to give examples of situations in which people give excuses or blame others rather than taking responsibility themselves.

3. Explain that one effective way to "stop the blame game" is to ask open-ended questions when people blame other people or situations for their own actions (or inaction).

4. Distribute the *Stopping the Blame Game Worksheet* to participants and ask them to work in pairs (or small groups) to complete the worksheet.

5. Tell them that they are to respond to each statement with an open-ended question that "forces" the other person to take responsibility for his or her actions (or inactions), but, at the same time, prevents any embarrassment to the individual. Give them 15 minutes.

6. At the end of the 15 minutes, reconvene the entire group and solicit examples of open-ended questions from the pairs (or subgroups). Suggested responses to the worksheet statements are as follows:

   1. What is your understanding of your job responsibilities?
   2. What leads you to believe that he should know how to do it?
   3. What can you do to compensate for the staff shortage?
   4. What is your degree of responsibility in this situation?
   5. What could you have done differently to make sure you had enough time?

6. What could you have done to make sure you were clear about what you needed to do?

7. How did you determine your priorities?

Discussion:

1. How difficult was it to develop open-ended questions?

2. What made it difficult or easy?

3. How was this approach similar to or different from what you would normally say?

4. What did you learn from the activity?

5. How can this help you in your own situations?

Variations:

• If time is limited, you may choose to assign one or two items from the worksheet to each pair (or subgroup) rather than asking them to do them all.

• You can use the examples of excuses participants offered in addition to or in place of the ones on the worksheet.

STOPPING THE BLAME GAME WORKSHEET

People who avoid taking responsibility or being accountable for their actions (or inactions) engage in assigning blame and making excuses. It is a leader's responsibility to hold them accountable! Please respond to the following statements by asking open-ended questions that "force" the other person to take responsibility for his or her actions but, at the same time, prevent any embarrassment to the individual.

1. "It's not my job."

2. "He should know how to do it."

3. "We have a staff shortage."

4. "It's not my fault."

5. "I didn't have enough time."

6. "Your directions weren't clear."

7. "Other priorities got in the way."

TEAM MODELS

Competency: Team Building

Description: In this activity, participants explore the different sports team models and how those models relate to their work teams.

Goals:

- Distinguish among the four basic sports team models as they relate to workplace teams.
- Identify the types of teams participants currently lead.
- Determine how closely participants' teams resemble the types of teams they want to lead.

Time Required: 45 minutes

Materials and Preparation:

- *Team Models Worksheet* (one per participant)
- *Team Models* (one per participant)

Process:

1. Introduce the activity by explaining that many people use the concept of sports teams to make a point or conduct a discussion about workplace teams. Point out that although a sports team can be an interesting analogy for a workplace team, we must take into consideration that different sports have different models in terms of structure and the degree of player interaction and interdependence.
2. Divide the group into subgroups of four or five and distribute a copy of the *Team Models Worksheet* to each participant. Ask the groups to describe the makeup or structure of each type of team, particularly focusing on the relationship of team members to each other as well as the degree of interaction and interdependence among the team members. Give them 20 minutes.
3. At the end of the 20 minutes, call time and reconvene the group. Ask for volunteers to share their worksheet responses. Distribute the *Team Models* handout and facilitate a discussion about the differences among the four team models as well as their application to workplace teams.
4. Then ask the participants each to think about their own work team and write down which one of the sports team models best describes their team and why. Give them 7 or 8 minutes. Use the following questions to provoke their thinking:
   - Which type of team most closely resembles your work team?

(Continued)

- What is the reason you chose this particular team model as representative of your team?
- Describe the structure of your team.
- To what degree do your team members interact with each other?
- How interdependent are your team members?

5. At the end of the time period, ask them to work in pairs or small groups to discuss their responses with each other. Give them 10 minutes.

6. At the end of the 10 minutes, reconvene the group to conduct a general discussion.

Discussion:

1. What is your reaction to the type of team you have identified as your workplace team?
2. How pleased are you with the type of team your group models?
3. Would you prefer a different model for your team? Why or why not?
4. If you would prefer a different model, what can you do to create that type of team?

Variations:

- You may choose to divide the group into four subgroups and assign each of the four groups a different team model. If you use this variation, eliminate steps 4 and 5.
- If participants are from the same organization, you may ask them to identify and discuss which type of team their organization models. This would be done throughout the activity.

TEAM MODELS WORKSHEET

For each type of team, describe the following: the structure (relationship of team members to each other), the degree of interaction among team members, and the degree of interdependence among team members.

	Track	Baseball	Football	Basketball
Structure				
Member Interaction				
Interdependence				

TEAM MODELS WORKSHEET SAMPLE

	Track		Football	Basketball
Structure	Members work independently.	Members are relatively independent; assigned to specific positions.	Members are divided into three subteams; assigned to specific positions.	Members are involved in all aspects of the game; play on the team as a whole.
Member Interaction	Little or no interaction	Some interaction	Interaction centered within subteams	High degree of interaction
Interdependence	No interdependence	Some interdependence	Interdependence within subteams	High level of interdependence

THE MAGIC OF MENTORING

Competency: Mentoring

Description: The purpose of this activity is for the participants to explore the value of the mentor-mentee relationship and consider how they can develop mentoring relationships.

Goals:

- Identify the skills, qualities, and traits of an effective mentor.
- Recognize the role of a mentor in helping a person's career.

Time Required: 30–40 minutes

Materials and Preparation:

- Flip chart pages or slides with one of the following questions on each:
  - *Round 1:* Has anyone been a mentor to you? What did the person do? What was the relationship like?
  - *Round 2:* Have you been a mentor to someone else? What did you do for the person? What was the relationship like?
  - *Round 3:* What are the skills, qualities, and traits of an effective mentor?
- Blank flip chart pages
- Markers

Process:

1. Introduce the activity by mentioning that mentoring has been used throughout the ages to nurture and develop others. Mentoring is an important leadership competency.
2. Ask the participants to name famous real or fictional mentor-mentee relationships and capture these pairings on flip chart pages. Some examples may include to following:

Mentor	Mentee
Obi-Wan Ben Kenobi	Luke Skywalker (*Star Wars*)
Merlin	King Arthur
Socrates	Plato
Johnny Carson	Jay Leno
Walter Cronkite	Dan Rather
Peter Drucker	Jim Collins
Andrew Carnegie	Charles Schwab
Isaac Asimov	Gene Roddenberry

(Continued)

3. Provide a definition of mentoring: it involves "a relationship in which a person with greater experience, expertise, and wisdom counsels, teaches, guides and helps another person to develop both personally and professionally" (Shea, 1992).

4. Briefly discuss the importance of mentoring in today's workplace, pointing out that mentoring is about building a relationship of trust between the mentor and mentee.

5. Explain that participants are going to explore the various skills, qualities, and traits of effective mentors.

6. Divide the group into trios. Position the trios in the room so that each trio can clearly see the other trios on either side of them.

7. Post the questions for Round 1 (Has anyone been a mentor to you? What did the person do? What was the relationship like?) and ask members of the trios to discuss the questions by sharing their personal experiences. Give them 5 minutes.

8. At the end of the 5 minutes, call time and ask the trios to assign a 0, 1, or 2 to each person in the trio. Direct the participants with the number 1 to move one trio clockwise, and those with the number 2 to move two trios clockwise. Ask the participants with the number 0 to remain seated. They will be permanent members of a trio site.

9. Post the questions for Round 2 (Have you been a mentor to someone else? What did you do for the person? What was the relationship like?) and begin the discussion. Again, give them 5 minutes.

10. Call time and repeat the movement process identified in step 8.

11. Post the question for Round 3 (What are the skills, qualities, and traits of an effective mentor?) and give them another 5 minutes to discuss the question.

12. At the end of Round 3, call time and reconvene the group. Conduct a discussion about the skills, qualities, and traits of an effective mentor and capture those items on a flip chart page.

Discussion:
1. What was your reaction to the discussion of mentor experiences?
2. What did you learn about being a mentor?
3. How is mentoring used in your organization?
4. How can you develop mentoring relationships?

Variation:
• Instead of conducting a rotating trio exchange, divide the group into subgroups of three or four and have each group answer all three questions.

WHAT DO YOU EXPECT?

Competency: Clarifying Expectations

Description: This role-play activity gives participants the opportunity to clarify and communicate job performance expectations.

Goals:

- Identify the importance of clarifying and communicating performance expectations.
- Follow a three-step process for clearly communicating performance standards and expectations.

Time Required: 60 minutes

Materials and Preparation:

- *Manager Instructions—Round 1* (one per trio)
- *Manager Instructions—Round 2* (one per trio)
- *Manager Instructions—Round 3* (one per trio)
- *Clarifying Expectations Observer Sheet* (one per participant)

Process:

1. Introduce the activity by explaining the importance of communicating clear performance expectations to employees. When employees know what is expected of them, they are more motivated to meet those expectations. Exceptional leaders communicate and measure performance in precise, objective terms. They specify speed (rate), quantity (number or amount), accuracy (absence of errors), thoroughness (completeness), and timelines (deadlines to be met). Furthermore, they focus on the positive performance they want rather than the negative consequences of a failure to perform.

2. Ask participants for examples of specific types of expectations or standards of performance a leader might communicate to an employee, such as sales goals, production output, and so on.

3. Mention that this communication should occur well before the person's performance appraisal. Ideally it should take place the first day a new employee comes on board; however, it's never too late to start. At the very least, the leader should clearly state at the end of the current performance appraisal interview his or her expectations of the employee's performance for the next review period.

(Continued)

4. Tell participants they will have an opportunity to practice clarifying and communicating expectations. Explain that the role-play will consist of three 5-minute rounds, and that each person will have a chance to experience the roles of manager, employee, and observer.

5. Distribute the *Clarifying Expectations Observer Sheet* to each participant and review each step in the process, citing specific examples to illustrate each step. For instance, an expectation for each employee (regardless of position or location) is that he or she is responsible for maintaining the cleanliness and neatness of the office or department in which he or she works, including the individual's own work station. This is important because it relates to customers' perceptions of the organization. It also contributes to a healthy, safe, and pleasant work environment (Step 1). Each employee is expected to keep his or her workstation free of clutter and put client files in drawers at the end of each day (Step 2). The appearance of the employee's work area will be monitored on a regular basis and will be a part of the employee's review process (Step 3).

6. Divide participants into subgroups of three. Ask them to identify which role each person would like for each round. Then distribute the instructions for managers to each group. Each person in a trio receives different manager instructions.

7. Explain that when they are in the employee's role, they should be as realistic as possible. Give managers 5 minutes to review their manager instructions and prepare for the role-play using their own specific standards and expectations.

8. At the end of the 5 minutes, tell them to begin Round 1 of the role-play.

9. At the end of the 5 minutes, stop the role-play and ask each observer to give feedback to the manager as to how well he or she clarified and communicated his or her expectations to the employee. Allow 10 minutes.

10. Repeat the process for Round 2 and Round 3.

11. Following the Round 3 feedback, reconvene the entire group and conduct a general discussion of the activity and what they learned.

Discussion:

1. How did it feel to be in the manager's role?
2. How did it feel to be in the employee's role?
3. How difficult was it to cite specific standards and expectations?
4. How is the approach similar to or different from what you currently do?
5. What are you going to do differently in the future?
6. How can this help you be a more effective leader?

Variations:
- Instead of asking each manager to identify the performance standards for each job duty or responsibility, you could create descriptions of standards and expectations specific to your organization.
- Instead of having managers focus on a customer contact position, as specified in their instructions, you could ask each manager to identify performance criteria for a position of his or her choice.

MANAGER INSTRUCTIONS—ROUND 1

You will be communicating your expectations and standards of performance to an employee in a primary customer contact position. You will tell the employee how he or she should behave in a face-to-face situation with an external customer.

MANAGER INSTRUCTIONS—ROUND 2

You will be communicating your expectations and standards of performance to an employee in a primary customer contact position. You will tell the employee how he or she should behave when interacting with an external customer on the telephone.

MANAGER INSTRUCTIONS—ROUND 3

You will be communicating your expectations and standards of performance to an employee in regard to his or her interactions with coworkers in his or her own department and throughout the organization. You will be stressing the importance of internal customer service.

CLARIFYING EXPECTATIONS OBSERVER SHEET

As you observe the manager-employee interaction, pay careful attention to how well the manager follows each step. Please note specific words or phrases the manager used during that step.

Step 1: Review the duty and responsibility, including how this responsibility fits into the "big picture."

Step 2: State specific performance standards and expectations, quantifying if possible.

Step 3: Explain how and when the performance will be evaluated.

WHAT MENTORS DO

Competency: Mentoring

Description: This activity is designed to help participants explore the behaviors of effective mentors and the impact mentors have on mentees and their careers.

Goals:

- Identify the behaviors of effective mentors.
- Assess participants' own mentor behaviors.

Time Required: 30 minutes

Materials and Preparation:

- *What Mentors Do* (one per participant)
- Flip chart pages
- Markers

Process:

1. Introduce the activity by asking participants to think about mentors they have had. Ask them to work with a partner and list the skills or competencies they think are important for a mentor to demonstrate in order to be effective. Give them 3 minutes.
2. At the end of the 3-minute period, reconvene the group and solicit input from the pairs, and post their suggestions on a flip chart page.
3. Hand out copies of *What Mentors Do* to the participants. Ask them to look at the list just distributed and compare it with the list on the flip chart. Note the similarities and differences.
4. Point out that the *What Mentors Do* list has two columns:

    As a mentee—what their mentors have done for them

    As a mentor—what they as mentors have done for others
5. Ask them to take 5 minutes and place check marks in the appropriate columns.
6. After 5 minutes, reconvene the group and ask for volunteers to share examples from each of the two lists.

Discussion:

1. What did you learn about the behaviors of effective mentors?
2. How did the behaviors of your own mentors help you?
3. What did you learn about yourself as a mentor?
4. How can you use this checklist in your role as a mentor?

Variation:

- You may want to use this activity in conjunction with the Magic of Mentoring activity. In that case, you would refer to the list of skills, qualities, and traits the group generated from that activity.

WHAT MENTORS DO QUESTIONNAIRE

First think about your experiences with those who have mentored you. With those experiences in mind, check the items under the "as a mentee" column that your mentors have done for you. Then think about your experiences as a mentor, and check the items under the "as a mentor" column that you have done for others.

	As a Mentee	**As a Mentor**
1. Shared his or her personal experiences as an employee of the organization	☐	☐
2. Discussed the mentee's career goals	☐	☐
3. Gave inside information on the organization's politics	☐	☐
4. Listened to the mentee's concerns	☐	☐
5. Gave feedback about the mentee's behavior, career plans, and performance	☐	☐
6. Involved the mentee in activities outside his or her job responsibilities	☐	☐
7. Encouraged the mentee to speak up, take the initiative, and take risks	☐	☐
8. Introduced the mentee to key people in the organization	☐	☐
9. Taught the mentee about the organization's culture, traditions, and values	☐	☐
10. Showed how to use the informal system to accomplish goals	☐	☐
11. Built the mentee's confidence by giving pep talks and positive reinforcement	☐	☐
12. Provided opportunities for the mentee to showcase his or her talents	☐	☐
13. Served as a role model of proper conduct and professional behavior	☐	☐
14. Facilitated learning and development opportunities	☐	☐
15. Helped the mentee self-assess	☐	☐
16. Offered career advice	☐	☐

	As a Mentee	As a Mentor
17. Took a personal interest in the mentee's life	☐	☐
18. Provided access to information not usually available to the mentee	☐	☐
19. Set high expectations	☐	☐
20. Challenged the mentee	☐	☐
21. Coached the mentee	☐	☐
22. Supported the mentee when he or she made a mistake	☐	☐
23. Offered encouragement	☐	☐

CHAPTER EIGHT

INCREASING LEADERSHIP EFFECTIVENESS

This chapter primarily focuses on developing the characteristics and competencies that increase the leader's effectiveness. The activities center on fostering relationships, exercising good judgment, maintaining a clear focus, making decisions, and solving problems. They also address developing intangible qualities, such as by becoming more resilient and confident.

BOUNCING BACK

Competency: Resilience

Description: This visualization exercise is designed to help participants use a stress-management technique to become more resilient when faced with the pressures they encounter in both their personal and professional lives.

Goals:

- Use a relaxation technique to manage stress.
- Identify the importance of resilience as a leadership characteristic.

Time Required: 20 minutes

Materials and Preparation:

- Recording of soft classical music or environmental sounds, such as a babbling brook or ocean waves breaking on the shore
- Equipment to play the recording

Process:

1. Introduce the activity by discussing resilience and its importance as a leadership characteristic. Explain that effective leaders demonstrate resilience by dealing with pressure, remaining optimistic, and recovering quickly from setbacks. Point out that resilience is related to stress management.

2. Solicit from the group examples of behaviors they practice to help reduce or manage their stress. Examples might include exercising, getting adequate sleep, maintaining proper eating habits, meditating, receiving massage therapy, and so on.

3. Explain that you are going to have them practice a stress-reducing relaxation technique. This is an exercise that only takes 10 minutes, and they can do it any place at any time.

4. Turn down the lights, start the music, and ask the participants to get comfortable (for example, by loosening their belts or removing their shoes).

5. Use the following script:

   "Think about a place where you go to relax or rest. Visualize yourself there.

   - What are you wearing?
   - What do you see?
   - What do you hear?
   - What do you smell?

- What time of day is it?
- What time of year is it?
- Where are you sitting?
- What do you feel?

"Close your eyes and breathe slowly in and out. Focus on breathing deeply from your diaphragm. Inhale slowly and deeply for 4 seconds, counting 1, 2, 3, 4 in your head. Now exhale slowly for 4 seconds. Picture yourself in your special place as you concentrate on breathing in and out.

"As you continue breathing deeply, listening to the relaxing, soothing sounds, and picturing yourself in your special place, focus your attention on your muscle groups. Begin by tensing the muscles in your feet, holding the tension, and then relaxing the muscles, and continue this process with every muscle group, moving up through the body to the face, neck, and head.

"Continue to breathe deeply. As you breathe in, mentally say to yourself, 'I am . . .' And as you breathe out, say to yourself, '. . . relaxed.' Continue breathing in and out and mentally reciting this   mantra for the next few minutes." (Note: Give them 5 to 8 minutes to practice the relaxation technique.)

6. At the end of the time period, ask them to open their eyes, while you slowly bring up the lights and discontinue the music.

Discussion:
1. How do you feel (even though this is an artificial situation)?
2. How can you use this exercise to help you?
3. What are some examples of times when resilience is needed in a work setting?

Variation:
- You can also use a prerecorded relaxation script.

DISTINGUISHING BEHAVIORS

Competency: Confidence

Description: This card sort activity is designed to help participants understand the essence and power of assertive behaviors.

Goals:
- Identify the differences among assertive, aggressive, passive, and passive-aggressive behaviors.
- Gain insight into participants' own patterns of behaviors.

Materials and Preparation:
- Refer to the *Distinguishing Behaviors Card Sort Answer Sheet* and create Card Sort sets (one set per group) as follows: on unlined, three-by-five index cards, create "header" cards by putting each of the following words on a separate card: "Aggressive," "Assertive," "Passive," and "Passive-Aggressive." Create "descriptor" cards for each of the above "header" cards. Each descriptor goes on a separate card.
- *Distinguishing Behaviors Card Sort Answer Sheet* (one per participant)

Process:
1. Divide participants into subgroups of five or six people.
2. Give each group a stack of cards that has been shuffled.
3. Explain that the deck of cards consists of four "header" cards and twenty-four "descriptor" cards. Each team's task is to sort the descriptor cards into the appropriate headings or categories. Tell them that there are six descriptor cards for each category. Allow approximately 10 minutes.
4. At the end of the 10 minutes, ask the teams to stop working, and distribute the answer sheet. Ask the teams to "score" themselves by determining how many they placed in the correct category.
5. After they have determined how well they did, ask each team to share its results with the rest of the group.
6. Ask for volunteers to summarize their understanding of each of the four types of behaviors.

Discussion:
1. What did you experience as you were working together to sort the cards?
2. Was there any evidence of these behaviors in your group?

3. What are some examples of times when you have demonstrated these behaviors in your own professional or personal situations?

4. What are some specific situations that would require you to use each one of these behaviors?

5. How can this information help you in your daily interactions with others?

Variation:

• To help participants experience these four types of behaviors after they have identified them, divide the group into four subgroups and assign each subgroup a different category of behaviors. Also, identify realistic business-related scenarios to which they can apply these behaviors, such as asking the boss for a raise, delegating an unpleasant assignment to an employee, or asking an employee to work longer hours. Choose one or more of these scenarios (or use your own) and give the subgroups 5 to 10 minutes to practice role-playing the scenario to demonstrate their assigned behaviors. Reconvene the group and have each subgroup role-play its assigned behaviors for the rest of the group.

DISTINGUISHING BEHAVIORS CARD SORT ANSWER SHEET

Aggressive
- Usurps others' rights
- Makes abrupt gestures, points fingers
- Interrupts; dominates; is authoritarian
- Stares; talks loudly; invades others' space
- Has stiff and rigid posture
- Blames; accuses; attacks; demands; uses "you" statements

Assertive
- Maintains own rights
- Has direct gaze, varied voice, and balanced stance
- Is open, direct, and honest
- Allows others to express their feelings
- Has firm, warm, and relaxed voice
- Speaks own mind openly and directly; uses "Let's . . ." "We could . . ." "I want [need, expect, would prefer] . . ." and "How can we . . .?" statements

Passive
- Gives up own rights—allows others to choose
- Averts gaze; speaks softly; draws back
- Is insecure, apologetic, and hesitant
- Nods head excessively; makes nervous gestures
- Holds feelings inside or expresses them indirectly
- Qualifies; apologizes; questions; uses "Is it okay . . . ?" "Do you mind if . . . ?" and "Could I . . . ?" statements

Passive-Aggressive
- Sneaks to usurp others' rights
- Casts sideways glances; shifts body
- Speaks sarcastically
- Uses indirect put-downs
- Manipulates others
- Is outwardly agreeable yet does not comply

Source: "Distinguishing Behaviors" by Karen Lawson in *SkillBuilders: 50 Communication Skills Activities.*
Copyright © 2000 by HRDQ.

EMPLOYEE DEVELOPMENT DECISIONS

Competency: Decision Making

Description: This case study activity helps participants create a structured process for making decisions.

Goals:

- Distinguish between decision making and problem solving.
- Develop a process for making decisions.

Time Required: 45–60 minutes

Materials and Preparation:

- *Case Study: Whom Do We Send to Training?* (one per participant)
- Flip chart pages
- Markers
- Masking tape

Process:

1. Begin by explaining that a leader's ability to make decisions is a critical part of his or her responsibility, and that quite often leaders make decisions with little information or without a well-thought-out process.

2. Explain that the terms *decision making* and *problem solving* are not synonymous. Decision making is part of problem solving, and involves choosing what to do about a problem or situation. Any situation in which there are choices, alternatives, or options calls for a decision. Decision making is making a conscious choice directed toward achieving an objective.

3. Ask the group for examples of everyday personal decisions they must make (such as what to wear, where to dine, what to watch on TV, or how to get to work). Then ask for work-related examples. Encourage them to offer employee-related examples.

4. Tell them that one of the important decisions leaders have to make relates to employee development. Explain that they will have an opportunity to experience a structured approach to decision making through a case study in which they will work in small groups to decide whom they would send to a supervisory training program.

(Continued)

5. Divide the group into subgroups of five to seven. Distribute a copy of the case study to each participant. Provide background for the case study by reading the first paragraph.

6. Tell them that they have 30 minutes to identify the criteria they will use to decide who should receive training and then select which employees they will send to the supervisory training program. They are to create a matrix on flip chart paper and post it on the wall after they have arrived at their decision. They should also be prepared to explain and defend their choices. Although you will not identify criteria for them, some examples of criteria include the following: (1) need and performance, (2) workload, (3) experience and seniority, (4) interest, (5) size of staff, and (6) prior training and education.

7. At the end of the 30 minutes, ask the subgroups to post their matrices on the wall, and then ask a spokesperson from each subgroup to explain their reasons for choosing the employees they identified to attend the training program.

8. Compare the lists and note the similarities and differences. Point out that there are no right or wrong answers.

Discussion:

1. What did you experience during this activity as you were trying to identify the criteria and then evaluate the candidates according to those criteria?

2. How was the process you used similar to or different from the way in which you would normally have made the decision?

3. What are some decisions you have made or expect to make for which you could apply this process?

4. How will this process help you with future decisions?

Variations:

- In a multisession program, you could give this as an individual or group assignment between sessions.

- You can use this as an individual assignment in a coaching situation.

- To save time, you could create the matrix and give it to the participants, rather than asking them to develop one of their own.

CASE STUDY: WHOM DO WE SEND TO TRAINING?

SCENARIO

You and your colleagues are members of a committee responsible for identifying supervisors to attend a nine-session supervisory training program. You have nine supervisors from various departments who are being considered; however, due to budgetary constraints, you can only select four people.

Gwen, Andrew, and Karen have been in supervisory positions for eight to ten years. Both Andrew and Karen have expressed an interest in attending the program. Although Andrew has had no formal training in supervisory skills, he has shown some natural leadership ability. Karen, however, is experiencing a number of employee problems in her department, including high turnover. Both have a fairly large staff of fifteen to twenty people they directly supervise.

Bob and Ann could definitely use the training, but both have a staff shortage, and their departments are responsible for a number of important projects with tight deadlines. Both of them have been identified as high potentials. They are eager to do whatever it takes to get the job done, even if it means "rolling up their sleeves" and doing many of the tasks themselves. Bob has "come up through the ranks" and performed many of the jobs he is now overseeing. Ann was recruited from a competing company.

Jessica and Alex are also good candidates for the training. Jessica has been a supervisor for a total of five years, two of which were in another organization, where she started as a management trainee. Alex has been a supervisor for four years and recently received his MBA. Despite his formal education, Alex has a reputation for managing by control and intimidation.

Abby and Jeff have been supervisors for less than a year. They are energetic and enthusiastic, and their employees speak highly of them. Your concern, however, is that they are perhaps too friendly with their employees, often partying with their employees after work and relying on group consensus to make all decisions. Jeff has indicated that he would like more responsibility, and often volunteers for additional assignments.

Your committee must decide who will attend the supervisory training program. Although your budget can accommodate four participants, you do not have to send four people.

(Continued)

ASSIGNMENT

1. Identify the criteria you will use to decide who will participate in the supervisory training program (for example, seniority). Don't be limited by the information presented in the case. You may decide there are other criteria you would use that are not obvious, but may be important to making your decision. Choose the top three to six most important criteria and rank them in order of importance.

2. Create a matrix that lists the names of the employees and also the criteria. Then decide on a rating system for each criterion as it applies to each employee. You may choose to rate each employee using "high," "medium," or "low," or perhaps you would like to use a numbering system, assigning point values. It's your choice.

3. Once you have created the matrix and agreed on the relative importance of the different criteria, choose the people you would send to the training program and be prepared to explain and justify your decision.

FIGURE IT OUT

Competency: Problem Solving

Description: This activity gives participants an opportunity to apply decision-making techniques to their own job situations.

Goals:

- Identify the steps in the decision-making process.
- Apply a decision-making model to a current situation.

Time Required: 45 minutes

Materials and Preparation:

- *Problem Worksheet* (one per participant)
- Flip chart page
- Markers

Process:

1. Introduce the activity by explaining that a problem exists when there is a gap between the current situation and the desired situation. Provide an example, such as a staff shortage, and ask for examples of work-related problems participants are experiencing or have experienced. Post their responses on a flip chart page. (Examples include high error rates, missed deadlines, equipment failures, and customer problems.)

2. Distribute the *Problem Worksheet.* Explain that good leaders follow a systematic process to solve problems. Using the example of the staff shortage problem (or another of your choosing), refer participants to the *Problem Worksheet* and work through the problem as a group.

3. Next explain that they will have an opportunity to apply the process to their own problems. Ask them to think of a problem that is facing them right now. Working individually, they are to use the worksheet to identify causes and possible solutions. If they cannot think of a current problem, they can think of one they have already solved; however, they should not think of how they actually solved it, but rather how they would approach it following the process outlined in the worksheet. Give them 30 minutes.

4. At the end of the 30 minutes, reconvene the group and ask them to share their experience using the structured process. If time permits, ask for a few volunteers to each share their problem and solution with the entire group.

(Continued)

Discussion:

1. What was your reaction to following this process?
2. What were some of the barriers you encountered as you worked through the problem?
3. How was this approach different from or similar to what you have done in the past?
4. How will you use this approach in the future?
5. How do you expect this process to help you when you are faced with problems?

Variations:

- Rather than work through the sample problem as a large group, you could create subgroups and ask each subgroup to work through the process.
- Instead of having participants work individually, you can create subgroups and assign each one a different problem from the list generated in step 1. Each subgroup could capture its problem-solving process on a flip chart page and post it on the wall.
- You can use this in an individual coaching session.
- In a multisession program, this can be used as an intersession individual assignment.

PROBLEM-SOLVING WORKSHEET

The following is a step-by-step process for solving problems.

1. Briefly describe the problem (the difference between the current situation or condition and the desired situation or condition).

2. What is your objective?

3. List the steps you would take to gather information about the problem.

4. List the possible alternatives or solutions generated from information gathering, as well as possible outcomes for each.

5. Which alternative would you choose and why?

6. How would you implement your solution (who, what, when, how)?

7. How are you going to evaluate your solution?

INNOVATION OR CREATIVITY?

Competency: Innovation/Creativity

Description: This activity lets participants explore their own ability to think "outside the box" and discuss the importance of innovation and creativity to a leader's success.

Goals:

- Distinguish between creativity and innovation.
- Explain how creativity and innovation are related to leadership effectiveness.

Time Required: 45–60 minutes

Materials and Preparation:

- A variety of paper clips, rubber bands, and pipe cleaners
- Flip chart pages
- Markers
- Masking tape

Process:

1. Divide the group into three subgroups.
2. Give one subgroup paper clips; another subgroup, rubber bands; and the third subgroup, pipe cleaners.
3. Ask subgroups each to make a list of all the uses they can think of for the item they have been assigned. They are to come up with new, creative, and innovative ideas and write these on flip chart paper. Give them 10 minutes.
4. At the end of the 10 minutes, ask them to post their flip chart pages on the wall.
5. Review each list for the number of items and most creative ideas. Ask each subgroup to identify its most creative idea.
6. Ask subgroup members to discuss among themselves the difference between creativity and innovation and to be able to explain how the items on their list are examples of creativity, innovation, or both. Give them 5 minutes.
7. At the end of the 5 minutes, solicit their ideas and post these on a flip chart page.
8. Present a lecturette in which you distinguish between creativity and innovation. Explain that Theodore Levitt, a former editor of the *Harvard Business Review (HBR)*, made a distinction between creativity and innovation in the classic 1963 *HBR* article titled "Creativity Is Not Enough." To paraphrase Levitt, in essence, creativity is thinking up new ideas, and innovation is doing new things, that is, putting the ideas into action. You

may want to mention that some authors and theorists use the two words interchangeably; others reverse the distinction between the two. For our purposes, *innovation* is taking ideas and putting them into action in the form of new products and services.

9. With that as a background, ask each subgroup to evaluate its most creative idea from the list according to a set of criteria that they will establish. Emphasize that innovation involves value, usefulness, and action. Give them 20 minutes.

10. At the end of the 20 minutes, reconvene the entire group and ask subgroup members to report how innovative they determined their idea to be.

Discussion:

1. What did you learn from the activity?

2. How is your understanding of innovation and creativity similar to or different from your ideas and definitions of the terms prior to participating in this activity?

3. How do innovation and creativity relate to a leader's success?

4. How can your understanding of innovation and creativity help you in your own development as a leader?

Variation:

• If time is limited, rather than having the groups evaluate their ideas, select the best idea from one of the groups and conduct a general discussion about its value and usefulness.

INTO THE FUTURE

Competency: Visioning

Description: This is an individual activity designed to help participants better understand the importance of creating a clear vision and communicating it to their employees.

Goals:

- Distinguish between a vision and a mission.
- Create vision statements for participants' departments or organizations.
- Explain how a vision can inspire and motivate others.

Time Required: 60–75 minutes

Materials and Preparation:

- *Into the Future Worksheet* (one per participant)

Process:

1. Begin by explaining that great leaders have a vision for their organization.
2. Ask participants (in pairs or as individuals) to explain the difference between vision and mission. Solicit responses and compare them with the following definitions:
   - A vision is a mental picture of what the organization should look like, feel like, and be seen as in the future.
   - A mission is a general description of why the organization (or department) exists. In other words, it identifies the function (products and services); those for whom the organization serves this function (customers or clients); and how the organization goes about filling this function (activities, technology, methods, and processes).
3. Ask participants if their respective organizations have a vision statement. If so, ask for volunteers to state their organization's vision.
4. Point out that although the organization as a whole may have a vision statement, it is important that a leader at any level should have a vision for his or her department or area of responsibility.
5. Explain that this activity is designed to give them an opportunity to think about and create a vision for their own department. Point out that a department vision must relate to the organization's vision.
6. Distribute a copy of the *Into the Future Worksheet* to each participant. Review the instructions and then give them 15 to 20 minutes to complete the worksheet.

7. At the end of the time period, create subgroups of four or five and ask participants to share their responses with their subgroup colleagues. Give them 25 minutes.

8. After 25 minutes, reconvene the entire group and discuss the outcome of the activity.

Discussion:

1. How difficult was it to answer the questions?
2. What made it easy or difficult?
3. What did you learn about creating a vision?
4. How can you use the vision you created in your role as a leader?
5. What are you going to do (or do differently)?

Variation:

- If participants are from the same organization or similar departments, you could create subgroups according to their commonalities and have them respond to the items on the worksheet as subgroups rather than as individuals. You could then have each subgroup record its vision on a flip chart page and post it on the wall.

INTO THE FUTURE WORKSHEET

Imagine that it is the year_____, five years after you and the other members of the leadership team created the vision for your organization (or department). The leadership team is meeting to reexamine and reevaluate that vision. In preparation for this meeting, each member has been asked to address the following questions:

1. How does the organization (or department) differ from what it was five years ago?

2. What specific changes have occurred in regard to the following (address all that would apply):
    - Products
    - Services
    - Employees
    - Customers and clients
    - Processes
    - Image
    - Technology
    - Market share
    - Financial position

3. What contributed to these changes?

4. What was the vision?

5. How did you communicate that vision to your employees, customers, shareholders, the public, and so on?

MAKING THE RIGHT CALL

Competency: Judgment

Description: The purpose of this activity is to help participants make good judgments about people.

Goals:

- Improve participants' judgment process.
- Apply the judgment process to hiring employees.

Time Required: 45–60 minutes

Materials and Preparation:

- *Behavioral Interviewing Basics* (one per participant)

Process:

1. Introduce the activity by explaining that the careers of many leaders have been built or destroyed by their judgment calls. Making the right calls about people is one of the most important areas in which good judgment is critical, particularly in hiring the right person for the right position at the right time. Also explain that there is a distinction between judgment and decision making. Decision making involves a single moment when the leader makes a decision. Judgment, however, is a process that unfolds over time.

2. Explain that the participants are going to have an opportunity to explore the beginning stages of the judgment process by first identifying intangible qualities and characteristics of the people they would like on their leadership team. They will then develop behavioral interviewing questions designed to elicit responses that will provide a basis for *judging* whether or not the candidate has the desired characteristics.

3. Distribute a copy of *Behavioral Interviewing Basics* to each participant. Review and explain the definition of behavioral interviewing: "the process by which the interviewer obtains behavioral information about past performance to predict the way an individual will perform in the future."

4. Explain that the first step in this process is to identify the desired qualities and characteristics and then structure behavior-based questions to determine the degree to which the candidate satisfies or meets each characteristic. Sample characteristics or qualities include interpersonal skills, initiative, flexibility, adaptability, integrity, teamwork, risk taking, and so on.

(Continued)

5. Review the model for structuring the questions:

   Situation   Background and context in which the candidate took action

   "Tell me about a time when . . . "

   Action   What the candidate did or said and how he or she did or said it

   "What did you do . . . ?"

   Result   Effects of the candidate's actions

   "What was the result of . . . ?"

6. Provide an example of a question designed to identify how the candidate deals with change, such as "Tell me about a time when you had to implement a change with which you completely disagreed. What did you do, and what was the result?" You may also want to solicit other examples from the group.

7. Divide the group into the number of characteristics you have (or the group has) identified. Please be sure you are focusing on intangible qualities rather than specific skills.

8. Assign each subgroup a different characteristic and ask the subgroups to develop one or two behavior-based questions that will uncover the candidate's strength or weakness in that area. Give them 10 minutes.

9. At the end of the 10 minutes, reconvene the entire group. Ask one of the subgroups to ask its question, and then solicit from individuals how they would answer the question if they were the candidate. After each response, discuss how well the answer provided the required information. Continue this process until all the characteristics have been addressed. (Note: As the facilitator you will need to make sure the questions follow the three-part format.)

10. At the end of the question-and-response period, conduct a discussion with the entire group focusing on how the responses would influence their judgment of the potential candidate. Point out that from the interviewer's perspective there is no right or wrong answer, and that different interviewers may judge the same candidate differently. Discuss the factors that influenced their reactions to the candidate's responses.

Discussion:

1. What was your reaction to developing the questions?

2. How did you feel when you had to give a response?

3. How were the questions in this activity similar to or different from those you would normally ask in an interview?

4. How would this type of questioning help you identify the right people for your team?

5. How are you going to adapt this approach to your own selection process?

Variations:

- Instead of having the participants answer each other's questions, you may choose to assume the role of the candidate and provide your own answers. After the mock interview is over, ask the subgroups to reconvene and prepare their assessment (or judgment) of the candidate. Have each subgroup share its assessment with the rest of the group.

- Rather than having the participants ask the questions to the entire group, put people into groups of three (with each person representing a different subgroup) and ask them to role-play within their trio, rotating the roles of interviewer, candidate, and observer. The observer would give feedback to the interviewer as to the effectiveness of his or her question.

Behavioral Interviewing Basics

The following offers a definition of behavioral interviewing as well as a model for constructing the questions to obtain the desired information about a candidate's past performance.

Definition of Behavioral Interviewing

Behavioral interviewing is the process by which the interviewer obtains behavioral information about past performance to predict the way an individual will perform in the future.

Developing Behavior-Based Questions

Situation   Background and context in which the candidate took action
   "Tell me about a time when . . ."

Action   What the candidate did or said and how he or she did or said it
   "What did you do?"

Result   Effects of the candidate's actions
   "What was the result of . . . ?"

NETWORKING CHECKLIST

Competency: Networking

Description: This checklist activity is designed to help participants evaluate their own networking skills and identify behaviors that will help them build valuable networks.

Goals:

- Identify behaviors that enhance networking success.
- Recognize the importance of developing networking skills.

Time Required: 15–20 minutes

Materials and Preparation:

- *Networking Checklist* (one per participant)

Process:

1. Introduce the activity by explaining that effective leaders are masters of networking. Recognized as the way to get things done in today's environment, networking involves various skills and activities that rely heavily on interpersonal communication. The people you meet and who become part of your network are valuable sources of information about your industry, your profession, other people, and even organizations. They are resources for gaining access to people and a source for referrals and business leads.

2. Ask participants to indicate by a show of hands how many use such social media networks as Facebook, LinkedIn, and Twitter. Ask them how they have benefited from those networks. Remind them that although social media is a very effective way of networking, the art of face-to-face networking is an important leadership competency.

3. Distribute the *Networking Checklist* and ask them to spend a few minutes responding "yes," "no," or "sometimes" by placing a check mark in the appropriate column.

4. After all participants have completed the inventory, reconvene the group and ask for volunteers to share examples of how they have practiced one or more of the items on the checklist. For example, you might solicit examples of the systems they use for noting "special information" about contacts, or ask them to share their experiences and involvement with professional organizations and how these have helped develop their leadership skills.

(Continued)

Discussion:

1. What did you learn about your face-to-face networking savvy?

2. What are some areas in which you would like to improve?

3. What are the advantages of face-to-face networking?

4. What are you going to do to improve your networking skills?

Variations:

• Ask the participants each to write down a networking action plan and share it with a partner or small group.

• You can enhance the activity by having the participants practice one or more of the items on the checklist, such as their 20-second self-introduction.

• This can be given as an individual assignment.

NETWORKING CHECKLIST

Check your networking savvy by asking yourself each of the following questions and placing a check mark in the appropriate column.

Do I . . .

Sometimes	**Yes**	**No**
1. Always carry business cards and practice business card etiquette?	☐	☐
2. Take every opportunity to meet new people no matter where I am?	☐	☐
3. Have a 20-second self-introduction that I can use in any situation?	☐	☐
4. Regularly attend meetings of professional organizations and get involved in committees and other activities?	☐	☐
5. Send congratulatory notes, memos, articles, and cartoons to people I have met as well as those I would like to meet?	☐	☐
6. Arrange networking breakfasts and lunches with my contacts on a regular basis?	☐	☐
7. Sit with people I don't know when attending a company or other business function?	☐	☐
8. Encourage people to talk about themselves by asking open-ended questions?	☐	☐
9. Listen actively by maintaining good eye contact, using positive body language, and paraphrasing as appropriate?	☐	☐
10. Know as much (or more) about the other person(s) as he/she/they know(s) about me at the end of a conversation?	☐	☐
11. Seek out and draw others into the conversation?	☐	☐
12. Follow up with a note or telephone call after I meet someone new?	☐	☐
13. Let people know I appreciate their help by sending cards or thanking them on the telephone?	☐	☐
14. Approach and introduce myself to small groups of strangers at social or business functions?	☐	☐
15. Have a system for recording contacts and noting "special information" about them?	☐	☐
16. Keep my word when I have promised to do a favor for someone?	☐	☐
17. Keep up-to-date on my reading concerning topics relevant to my business as well as in general subjects?	☐	☐

ON TARGET

Competency: Goal Setting

Description: In this activity, participants will explore the importance of setting specific goals, and they will have an opportunity to practice writing clear, concise, and complete goal statements.

Goals:

- Identify five goal-setting criteria.
- Write clear, concise, and complete goal statements.

Time Required: 40 minutes

Materials and Preparation:

- Flip chart page or slide that displays the following: "A goal is a statement of outcome and specific accountability that the person seeks to achieve over a specified period of time."
- *Goal-Setting Criteria* (one per participant)
- *Performance Standards* (one per participant)
- *Goal-Setting Worksheet* (one per participant)

Process:

1. Introduce the activity by telling the participants that setting goals is important to achieving success. Goal setting is a fundamental requirement in the process of performance management. People need to know what is expected of them and have some way to measure how well they are doing relative to the target.

2. Explain that participants are going to have an opportunity to practice writing clear, concise, and complete goal statements for both departmental and individual performance.

3. Display the slide or flip chart page showing the definition of a goal: "A goal is a statement of outcome and specific accountability that the person seeks to achieve over a specified period of time." Solicit examples of goals from the group.

4. Tell the group that a goal should have five criteria that fit the SMART acronym, and ask them what they are. Then distribute the *Goal-Setting Criteria* handout and review the criteria.

5. Emphasize the importance of "specific" and "measurable" and explain that those two criteria are related to performance standards. Distribute the *Performance Standards* handout and review it with the group.

6. Next divide the group into subgroups of two or four and distribute the *Goal-Setting Worksheet*. Ask them to write clear, concise, and complete goals following the five criteria. Give them 20 minutes.

7. At the end of the 20 minutes, reconvene the entire group and solicit examples of goals from the subgroups.

Discussion:

1. How difficult was it to write the goals following the five criteria?
2. What did you learn about writing goals that you didn't know before?
3. What is the benefit of writing clear, concise, and complete goals?
4. How can this help you in your role as a leader?

Variations:

- If time is limited, you may assign the departmental goals to half of the subgroups and the individual goals to the other half.
- You can ask the subgroups to work from their own examples of goals rather than using the ones on the *Goal-Setting Worksheet*.

GOAL-SETTING CRITERIA

Effective goals meet the five SMART criteria as identified below:

Specific: What task will be accomplished if the goal is achieved?

Measurable: What are the performance standards?

Attainable/Achievable: Do you have the ability to do it?

Realistic: Can it be done?

Time-bound: When is this goal to be achieved?

PERFORMANCE STANDARDS

Quality
- Degree of accuracy
- Maximum error rate
- Indicator of subjective satisfaction

Quantity
- Number
- Volume
- Rate
- Percentage
- Count
- Frequency

Time
- Length of time in seconds, minutes, hours, days, weeks, months
- Deadlines
- Temporal sequences ("before," "when," "after")

Cost
- Amount of money
- Budget
- Profit
- Cost of materials, resources

GOAL-SETTING WORKSHEET

Rewrite the following goal statements, making sure that each one reflects or adheres to the five criteria.

Departmental Goals

1. Improve response time.

2. Improve the quality of service.

3. Decrease the number of complaints.

4. Decrease costs.

5. Reduce overtime.

Individual Goals

1. Improve your error rate.

2. Improve your sales.

3. Improve your productivity.

4. Improve your job knowledge.

5. Improve your interpersonal skills.

SETTING PRIORITIES

Competency: Focus

Description: In this activity, participants are introduced to a system for prioritizing tasks, projects, or objectives.

Goals:

- Set realistic, results-oriented priorities.
- Distinguish between important and urgent as they relate to setting priorities.

Time Required: 30–40 minutes

Materials and Preparation:

- *Setting Priorities Rating System* (one per participant)

Process:

1. Begin the activity by explaining that effective leaders maintain focus by setting priorities so they can identify which projects or tasks need to be tackled first. Tell participants that this activity will provide a system for identifying priorities for themselves and others.

2. Explain that priorities are determined by two criteria: importance and urgency. Urgency relates to time or immediacy, and importance relates to value. Solicit examples of each from the group. An example of urgency would be a system failure; an example of importance might be establishing a customer relationship. Point out that managers often "lose their way" by focusing on what is urgent rather than on what is important.

3. Point out that it is often difficult to determine what to do first because there is a tendency to think everything is both urgent and important. Tell participants they are going to engage in an activity that will help them determine which projects or tasks should be addressed first in order to simplify the process of setting priorities.

4. Ask participants to work individually and list four or five tasks, projects, and so on that are currently on their "to do" list. Give them 10 minutes.

5. After each participant has made his or her list, distribute the *Setting Priorities Rating System* and explain how to use it by pointing out the point values under the "importance" and "urgency" columns. Demonstrate by soliciting an example of a project or task from the group and asking the group to assign "importance" and "urgency" numbers to the task. If no one has an example, you might offer one or more of the following:

   - Performance appraisals
   - Scheduling

(Continued)

- Customer calls
- Preparing next year's budget
- Employee coaching session

6. Ask the participants to return to their individual lists and use the rating system for each item.

7. After they have calculated the priority factor for each item, explain that they should list the tasks in descending order, indicating the order in which they should complete them. Tell them they have 10 minutes.

8. At the end of the 10 minutes, reconvene the group for a general discussion.

Discussion:

1. What was your reaction to using this system?
2. How difficult was it for you to assign numbers to "urgency" and "importance"?
3. How was this approach different from or similar to the one you normally take to determine priorities?
4. Which takes precedence: urgency or importance?
5. How might you use this system to help you maintain your focus?

Variation:

- After the participants have completed their priority ranking, ask them to work in pairs to share their lists and discuss how they arrived at their conclusions.

SETTING PRIORITIES RATING SYSTEM

Priorities are determined by two criteria: importance and urgency. Urgency relates to time or immediacy, and importance relates to value. To help you simplify the process of setting priorities, you will use the following system to determine the order in which you should approach your tasks.

Begin by listing four or five tasks or projects and then applying the rating system to each item on your list. Then list the tasks in descending order. The item with the highest number would be listed first. For tasks that receive the same score, use your judgment as to which one you are going to tackle first.

Importance

4 = Critical; must be done

3 = Very important; should be done

2 = Somewhat important; not really necessary but would be nice to do

1 = Relatively unimportant; no real consequences if it is not done

Urgency

4 = Must be done to avoid serious consequences

3 = Should be done soon

2 = Can be delayed

1 = Time not a factor

To Calculate the Priority Factor

Task/Project	Importance	×	Urgency	=	Total
		×		=	
		×		=	
		×		=	
		×		=	
		×		=	

THINGS WE HAVE IN COMMON

Competency: Relationship Building

Description: This activity stresses the importance of building relationships by capitalizing on the commonalities among people.

Goals:

- Recognize the importance of focusing on similarities when building relationships.
- Identify ways to uncover commonalities among people in a group.

Time Required: 10–15 minutes

Materials and Preparation:

- Flip chart pages
- Markers

Process:

1. Begin the activity by explaining that building relationships both inside and outside the organization is a key success factor for today's leaders. Tell participants they are going to have an opportunity to experience the basics of relationship building.
2. Divide the group into subgroups of five or six people. Ask the subgroups each to select a scribe and give a flip chart page and marker to that individual.
3. Ask people in each subgroup to come up with a list of things they all have in common (other than working for the same company, they are all sales reps, for example). Explain that each subgroup's official scribe will record the shared characteristics. The objective is to come up with as many similarities as possible within a limited amount of time. Give them 4 or 5 minutes.
4. Call time after 4 or 5 minutes. Survey the room for the subgroup that has the most items on its list. Ask the winning subgroup to share its list. Give prizes to the subgroup with the most items, or the most unusual item.
5. Discuss the importance of focusing on similarities rather than differences, and how that can be helpful in building relationships.

Discussion:

1. What process did you use for identifying the things you had in common?
2. What skills did you use to uncover your commonalities?

3. What did you learn about other people in your group?

4. How can you use this process in the future to build relationships?

Variation:

- You may choose to have the subgroups record their similarities on sheets of paper rather than flip chart pages.

TRUST ME

Competency: Trust Building

Description: In this activity, participants explore the concept of trust and the behaviors that can create trust (or mistrust) in a relationship.

Goals:

- Recognize the importance of developing and maintaining trusting relationships.
- Identify ways participants can earn trust from colleagues and followers.
- Identify ways participants can demonstrate trust in others.

Time Required: 30–40 minutes

Materials and Preparation:

- *Trust Me Worksheet* (one per participant)
- Flip chart page with the following T-chart: Earn Trust/Demonstrate Trust
- Markers

Process:

1. Introduce the activity by emphasizing that trust is a must in any relationship and in any organization. It is the basis from which all true leaders operate and is an essential element to organizational success. On the one hand, low levels of trust cause high levels of stress, reduce productivity, stifle innovation, and hamper the decision-making process. High levels of trust, on the other hand, increase employee morale; reduce absenteeism; promote innovation; and, perhaps most important, aid in managing change effectively. Building trust starts with creating a culture based on shared values. Maintaining trust requires a commitment to building interpersonal relationships based on honesty, integrity, and a genuine concern for others.

2. Explain that three different types of trusting relationships exist within any organization. A successful organization is built on a foundation that includes the following:

   Lateral trust—trust relations among peers or equals

   Vertical trust—trust relations between a supervisor and subordinate

   External trust—trust relations between an organization and its clients or suppliers

3. Emphasize that from a leadership perspective, trust works two ways. First, leaders must demonstrate the behaviors that can earn the *trust of others*. Second, effective leaders demonstrate *trust in others*.

4. Tell participants that in this activity they will be exploring specific behaviors that both earn trust and demonstrate trust.

5. Divide the group into subgroups of five or six and distribute the *Trust Me Worksheet* to the participants.

6. Tell them they have 15 minutes to develop two lists with these topics:
   - Things you can do to build trust
   - Things you can do to show you trust others

7. At the end of the 15 minutes, reconvene the entire group and solicit specific examples from the subgroups. Capture their responses on the T-chart (Earn Trust/Demonstrate Trust), and then discuss.

Discussion:

1. What insights did you gain about building and maintaining trusting relationships?

2. What did you learn about yourself?

3. How well do you practice the behaviors that earn and demonstrate trust?

4. What are you going to do (or do differently) to build and maintain trusting relationships?

5. How can this make you a more effective leader?

Variation:

- Ask half of the subgroups to develop the "Earn Trust" list, and the other half to compile the "Demonstrate Trust" list.

TRUST ME WORKSHEET

With the other members of your subgroup, identify *specific* behaviors leaders can practice that will create and maintain a climate of trust in the organization.

1. What can you do to earn the **trust of others**?

2. What can you do to demonstrate **trust in others**?

REFERENCES

Aesop's Fables (George Fyler Townsend, trans.). (1968). Garden City, NY: Doubleday.

Calvert, Gene. (1993). *Highwire Management: Risk-Taking Tactics for Leaders, Innovators, and Trailblazers.* San Francisco: Jossey-Bass.

Lawson, Karen. (2000). *SkillBuilders: 50 Communication Skills Activities.* King of Prussia, PA: HRDQ.

Lawson, Karen. (2002). The Balancing Act: An Activity for Creating Work-Life Balance. In Mel Silberman (ed.), *2002 Training and Performance Sourcebook* (pp. 21–27). New York: McGraw-Hill.

Lawson, Karen. (2008). Management Model for Change: Presenting Change to Employees. In Elaine Beich (ed.), *2008 Pfeiffer Annual: Consulting.* San Francisco: Pfeiffer.

Lawson, Karen. (2009). *The Trainer's Handbook, Updated Edition.* San Francisco: Pfeiffer.

Levitt, Theodore. (1963). Creativity Is Not Enough. *Harvard Business Review.*

O'Toole, James. (1995). *Leading Change: Overcoming the Ideology of Comfort and the Tyranny of Custom.* San Francisco: Jossey-Bass.

Shea, Gordon F. (1992). *Mentoring: A Practical Guide.* Menlo Park, CA: Crisp.

Thomas, David C., and Inkson, Kerr. (2009). *Cultural Intelligence: Living and Working Globally* (2nd edition). San Francisco: Berrett-Koehler.

INDEX

Discover more at Pfeiffer.com

- The best in workplace performance solutions for training and HR professionals

- Online assessments

- Custom training solutions

- Downloadable training tools, exercises, and content

- Training tips, articles, and news

- Author guidelines, information on becoming a Pfeiffer Partner, and much more

Discover more at www.pfeiffer.com

Pfeiffer Publications Guide

This guide is designed to familiarize you with the various types of Pfeiffer publications. The formats section describes the various types of products that we publish; the methodologies section describes the many different ways that content might be provided within a product. We also provide a list of the topic areas in which we publish.

FORMATS

In addition to its extensive book-publishing program, Pfeiffer offers content in an array of formats, from fieldbooks for the practitioner to complete, ready-to-use training packages that support group learning.

FIELDBOOK Designed to provide information and guidance to practitioners in the midst of action. Most fieldbooks are companions to another, sometimes earlier, work, from which its ideas are derived; the fieldbook makes practical what was theoretical in the original text. Fieldbooks can certainly be read from cover to cover. More likely, though, you'll find yourself bouncing around following a particular theme, or dipping in as the mood, and the situation, dictate.

HANDBOOK A contributed volume of work on a single topic, comprising an eclectic mix of ideas, case studies, and best practices sourced by practitioners and experts in the field.

An editor or team of editors usually is appointed to seek out contributors and to evaluate content for relevance to the topic. Think of a handbook not as a ready-to-eat meal, but as a cookbook of ingredients that enables you to create the most fitting experience for the occasion.

RESOURCE Materials designed to support group learning. They come in many forms: a complete, ready-to-use exercise (such as a game); a comprehensive resource on one topic (such as conflict management) containing a variety of methods and approaches; or a collection of like-minded activities (such as icebreakers) on multiple subjects and situations.

TRAINING PACKAGE An entire, ready-to-use learning program that focuses on a particular topic or skill. All packages comprise a guide for the facilitator/trainer and a workbook for the participants. Some packages are supported with additional media—such as video—or learning aids, instruments, or other devices to help participants understand concepts or practice and develop skills.

- *Facilitator/trainer's guide* Contains an introduction to the program, advice on how to organize and facilitate the learning event, and step-by-step instructor notes. The guide also contains copies of presentation materials—handouts, presentations, and overhead designs, for example—used in the program.

- *Participant's workbook* Contains exercises and reading materials that support the learning goal and serves as a valuable reference and support guide for participants in the weeks and months that follow the learning event. Typically, each participant will require his or her own workbook.

ELECTRONIC CD-ROMs and web-based products transform static Pfeiffer content into dynamic, interactive experiences. Designed to take advantage of the searchability, automation, and ease-of-use that technology provides, our e-products bring convenience and immediate accessibility to your workspace.

METHODOLOGIES

CASE STUDY A presentation, in narrative form, of an actual event that has occurred inside an organization. Case studies are not prescriptive, nor are they used to prove a point; they are designed to develop critical analysis and decision-making skills. A case study has a specific time frame, specifies a sequence of events, is narrative in structure, and contains a plot structure—an issue (what should be/have been done?). Use case studies when the goal is to enable participants to apply previously learned theories to the circumstances in the case, decide what is pertinent, identify the real issues, decide what should have been done, and develop a plan of action.

ENERGIZER A short activity that develops readiness for the next session or learning event. Energizers are most commonly used after a break or lunch to stimulate or refocus the group. Many involve some form of physical activity, so they are a useful way to counter post-lunch lethargy. Other uses include transitioning from one topic to another, where "mental" distancing is important.

EXPERIENTIAL LEARNING ACTIVITY (ELA) A facilitator-led intervention that moves participants through the learning cycle from experience to application (also known as a Structured Experience). ELAs are carefully thought-out designs in which there is a definite learning purpose and intended outcome. Each step—everything that participants do during the activity—facilitates the accomplishment of the stated goal. Each ELA includes complete instructions for facilitating the intervention and a clear statement of goals, suggested group size and timing, materials required, an explanation of the process, and, where appropriate, possible variations to the activity. (For more detail on Experiential Learning Activities, see the Introduction to the *Reference Guide to Handbooks and Annuals*, 1999 edition, Pfeiffer, San Francisco.)

GAME A group activity that has the purpose of fostering team spirit and togetherness in addition to the achievement of a pre-stated goal. Usually contrived—undertaking a desert expedition, for example—this type of learning method offers an engaging means for participants to demonstrate and practice business and interpersonal skills. Games are effective for team building and personal development mainly because the goal is subordinate to the process—the means through which participants reach decisions, collaborate, communicate, and generate trust and understanding. Games often engage teams in "friendly" competition.

ICEBREAKER A (usually) short activity designed to help participants overcome initial anxiety in a training session and/or to acquaint the participants with one another. An icebreaker can be a fun activity or can be tied to specific topics or training goals. While a useful tool in itself, the icebreaker comes into its own in situations where tension or resistance exists within a group.

INSTRUMENT A device used to assess, appraise, evaluate, describe, classify, and summarize various aspects of human behavior. The term used to describe an instrument depends primarily on its format and purpose. These terms include survey, questionnaire, inventory, diagnostic, survey, and poll. Some uses of instruments include providing instrumental feedback to group members, studying here-and-now processes or functioning within a group, manipulating group composition, and evaluating outcomes of training and other interventions.

Instruments are popular in the training and HR field because, in general, more growth can occur if an individual is provided with a method for focusing specifically on his or her own behavior. Instruments also are used to obtain information that will serve as a basis for change and to assist in workforce planning efforts.

Paper-and-pencil tests still dominate the instrument landscape with a typical package comprising a facilitator's guide, which offers advice on administering the instrument and interpreting the collected data, and an initial set of instruments. Additional instruments are available separately. Pfeiffer, though, is investing heavily in e-instruments. Electronic instrumentation provides effortless distribution and, for larger groups particularly, offers advantages over paper-and-pencil tests in the time it takes to analyze data and provide feedback.

LECTURETTE A short talk that provides an explanation of a principle, model, or process that is pertinent to the participants' current learning needs. A lecturette is intended to establish a common language bond between the trainer and the participants by providing a mutual frame of reference. Use a lecturette as an introduction to a group activity or event, as an interjection during an event, or as a handout.

MODEL A graphic depiction of a system or process and the relationship among its elements. Models provide a frame of reference and something more tangible, and more easily remembered, than a verbal explanation. They also give participants something to "go on," enabling them to track their own progress as they experience the dynamics, processes, and relationships being depicted in the model.

ROLE PLAY A technique in which people assume a role in a situation/scenario: a customer service rep in an angry-customer exchange, for example. The way in which the role is approached is then discussed and feedback is offered. The role play is often repeated using a different approach and/or incorporating changes made based on feedback received. In other words, role playing is a spontaneous interaction involving realistic behavior under artificial (and safe) conditions.

SIMULATION A methodology for understanding the interrelationships among components of a system or process. Simulations differ from games in that they test or use a model that depicts or mirrors some aspect of reality in form, if not necessarily in content. Learning occurs by studying the effects of change on one or more factors of the model. Simulations are commonly used to test hypotheses about what happens in a system—often referred to as "what if?" analysis—or to examine best-case/worst-case scenarios.

THEORY A presentation of an idea from a conjectural perspective. Theories are useful because they encourage us to examine behavior and phenomena through a different lens.

TOPICS

The twin goals of providing effective and practical solutions for workforce training and organization development and meeting the educational needs of training and human resource professionals shape Pfeiffer's publishing program. Core topics include the following:

Leadership & Management

Communication & Presentation

Coaching & Mentoring

Training & Development

E-Learning

Teams & Collaboration

OD & Strategic Planning

Human Resources

Consulting